D1554837

DAVID POLIZZI

SOLITARY CONFINEMENT

Lived experiences and ethical implications

POLICY PRESS SHORTS RESEARCH

First published in Great Britain in 2017 by

Policy Press
University of Bristol
1-9 Old Park Hill
Bristol
BS2 8BB
UK
t: +44 (0)117 954 5940
pp-info@bristol.ac.uk
www.policypress.co.uk

North America office:
Policy Press
c/o The University of Chicago Press
1427 East 60th Street
Chicago, IL 60637, USA
t: +1 773 702 7700
f: +1 773 702 9756
sales@press.uchicago.edu
www.press.uchicago.edu

© Policy Press 2017

British Library Cataloguing in Publication Data
A catalogue record for this book is available from the British Library.

Library of Congress Cataloging-in-Publication Data
A catalog record for this book has been requested.

ISBN 978-1-4473-3753-9 (hardcover)
ISBN 978-1-4473-3756-0 (ePub)
ISBN 978-1-4473-3757-7 (Mobi)
ISBN 978-1-4473-3754-6 (ePdf)

Cover design by Policy Press
Front cover: image kindly supplied by Fotolia
Printed and bound in the United States of America

Contents

Dedication

I would like to dedicate this text to all of the incarcerated individuals whom I encountered during my time with the Pennsylvania Department of Corrections, particularly those who were forced to endure the harsh isolation of solitary confinement. It is my hope that this inhumane practice will finally be brought to its appropriate end.

Acknowledgments

I would like to thank Anthony Amatrudo, Bruce Arrigo, Matthew Draper, and Michael Perlin for their helpful insight and suggestions as I wrote this text over the last few months. I am appreciative of both their friendship and the depth of their scholarly reflection. I would also like to thank Liesel my wife and Maddie my daughter for putting up with me during this time and giving me the support that allowed me to finish this project.

1
THE EXPERIENCE OF SOLITARY CONFINEMENT: SOME BEGINNING REFLECTIONS

Anyone with any serious interest in the ethical implications of the penitentiary system in the United States will, in rather short order, need to struggle with the difficult reality of the practice of solitary confinement. As a pre-doctoral clinical psychology intern with the Pennsylvania Department of Corrections (DOC), I was literally confronted by that reality during the very first week of that clinical placement. On entering the 400-bed segregated housing unit – a unit that housed both administrative and disciplinary custody inmates – I was struck by the austere surroundings of spit-shined concrete floors, the dimmed lighting, the 40-odd cells which rung each "state-of-the-art" pod and the shallow echoing of voices attempting to make contact with other inmates or staff from behind heavy steel doors.

Having worked with individuals coming out of the state system for approximately five years prior to entering the clinical psychology program at Duquesne University and prior to this clinical placement, I had listened as clients described what they euphemistically called the "hole." By the end of the first day of my clinical placement, however, it became abundantly clear that hearing about solitary confinement was not the same as experiencing these units firsthand. However, even that "reality check" paled in comparison to the reality for those individuals who were actually attempting to endure this experience.

During my very first visit to the segregation unit, I was introduced to the practice called "fishing." Fishing is the ingenious strategy developed by individuals on these units to communicate with each other from their individual cells; a communication that would be otherwise rather difficult or impossible to achieve. Each individual would fashion from the cloth threads taken from their prison uniforms a line that would be attached to some object, normally a matchbook cover that would serve as a hook; this hook would be attached to the line by some type of adhesive, normally a wad of gum. The line would then be tossed out from the space between the cell door and concrete floor, and sent in the direction of its intended recipient. The individual on the other end of this process would follow the same procedure and attempt to hook the line and in so doing create a single connection by which to communicate. Once the line was connected, individuals would use makeshift envelopes by which to send this "mail": play a back-and-forth game of chess, check on another inmate's well-being or simply engage in "conversation." Though technically viewed as a violation of disciplinary custody rules, it did not appear to be the case that this specific rule violation was rigidly enforced.

The practice of "fishing" represents an ingenious attempt to overcome the harsh environment of solitary confinement. Prohibited from any "normal" type of human interaction, the practice of "fishing" represents a successful attempt by the individual to reach out and establish a connection with another human being, while remaining physically isolated within the confines of an 8 by 12 cell. These contacts help to erode, at least for the moment, this experience of total isolation (O'Donnell, 2016). Fishing also reveals the vulnerability of such attempts, given that these relationships literally hang by a thread and can be easily disrupted. In such a deprived setting any success at establishing human contact was seen as a beneficial achievement.

Given the profound isolating effect of solitary confinement on these individuals, the possibility of participating in regular psychotherapy certainly had its advantages. The most general benefit offered was the ability to leave their cells for 30 or 40 minutes on a given day. Though the unit staff would have preferred that all "therapeutic interactions" take place at the cell door, I always insisted that the individual be removed from their cell and that we be provided a more or less private space where I could meet with them. However, this request hardly ensured that a "normal" client interaction would take place.

On meeting my first client, I was surprised by the fact that he was handcuffed and shackled at both the waist and feet. I recall naively asking if the cuffs could be removed during our sessions, but was quickly told that any inmate who is taken outside of his cell must be so confined. The circumstances, though not as absurd as attempting to provide psychotherapy within earshot of other individuals, certainly challenged my sense of what constituted a legitimate psychotherapeutic context. However, these more academic concerns quickly gave way to the more immediate need of creating a caring and respectful therapeutic frame, regardless the circumstances this context imposed.

During our initial meeting, I informed him that I had read his chart and was aware of the incident that had taken place in the county jail prior to his transfer to the state system. When I repeated the circumstances of that event as it was presented in the official misconduct, he immediately stated that the penitentiary's account was not true. He was then invited to share his side of the story. He began by explaining that it was true that a fist fight had occurred between him and another county jail inmate in the bathroom. He added that the fight was not very serious and was broken up by jail staff. However, he vehemently denied that he attempted to cut this individual's throat as the misconduct alleged. In fact, he invited me to contact the county jail myself and 'talk to Bob, he'll tell what happened.' Though I did privately question his description of events, I did not necessarily believe the account that was described in the misconduct. I did, however, know the individual he invited me to contact and would definitely be doing so in the next few days.

I was able to contact Bob the next day and discussed the case with him. I read him the written account as it was presented in the official misconduct and asked him to respond. 'Dave that is not what happened. I know this because the event took place on my pod and as supervisor, I was the one who investigated the incident.' He agreed with my client's account that a fight did take place, but denied that my client had attempted to slit the throat of the other individual. I ended our conversation by asking if he would be willing to talk with penitentiary administrators about this issue and he agreed to do so. Unfortunately that phone call never came.

As a result, I attempted to address this concern directly with penitentiary administrators. Unfortunately, every individual that I approached about this issue had the same response: 'You will need to take this up with my supervisor.' I was finally directed to the office of the assistant to the superintendent, who informed me that the situation was being explored. On the last week of my internship placement at that facility, I was informed by one of the full-time therapists that a process would be put in place to attempt to return the individual to general population. I left a few days later not knowing if the situation was ever resolved.

What is perhaps the most revealing and troubling aspect of the above account is the way in which solitary confinement was used to control a given inmate. The willingness of penitentiary administrators to fabricate the details of an event for the sole purpose of using that account to justify the decision to place this individual in disciplinary custody is not all that different from the type of rationale expected by inmates trying to "game the system." Such an action is in clear violation of Pennsylvania DOC regulations, which specifically prohibit placing an inmate in solitary confinement without legitimate, just cause to do so. When given the opportunity to correct this "error," prison administrators simply refused to contact the county jail supervisor or amend the "facts" that were described in the official misconduct and allowed the situation to remain unchanged. Unfortunately this is not the only example of the cavalier use of penitentiary administrative power.

On transferring to another site within the Pennsylvania system to complete my clinical internship, I was educated concerning another use of solitary confinement that could be viewed as more problematic than was the set of circumstances described in the previous account. Though, like the above account, it entailed the fabricating of an official misconduct, its purpose was intended to prevent an inmate from actually being released on parole from the penitentiary after that individual had received a release date from the state Office of Parole & Probation. The practice was well known to prison administrators, correctional officers, and inmates and was allowed to continue.

As one can imagine, the most anticipated letter an inmate could receive was the official confirmation of their release date from the penitentiary. Euphemistically known as the "green sheet," this announcement informed the individual of the exact date of their release. However, this notice also included the warning that if the individual was placed in disciplinary custody for any reason after the notice was issued, parole would be immediately revoked.

Though one's release date was often a tightly guarded "secret," this did not prevent correctional officers from sharing this information with other colleagues when it became available. One of the purposes of this "sharing" of information was to provide the opportunity for a given correctional officer(s) to basically circumvent the release date for this individual: If the officer felt that the individual "had not served enough prison time" or that they simply did not like the inmate in question, a bogus misconduct could be submitted, which would immediately nullify the individual's pending release. Such a result would require the inmate to serve an additional 12 months before they would once again be eligible for parole. Ironically enough, though this practice was an accepted aspect of penitentiary culture, there was a way to have this decision overturned.

Prior to any inmate being placed into disciplinary custody, a formal hearing would be convened to adjudicate the facts of the misconduct and determine the length of sentence for the given infraction. The individual would then be immediately sent to solitary if found guilty. These "green sheet misconducts" were no exception. In such circumstances, the inmate would be brought before the misconduct hearing officer where the "facts" of the case would be presented. However, unlike the more traditional misconduct hearing, a correctional officer could testify on the inmate's behalf and contest the legitimacy of the misconduct; as a result of this testimony, the inmate was normally found not guilty. If such testimony was not provided, the misconduct would stand and the individual would be sent to solitary and their parole would be rescinded.

What is so astounding about this process is that it was never truly corrected. Though it is true enough that the process described above did allow for a bogus misconduct to be overturned, there was never any institutional pressure to stop this type of behavior. The "corrective process" could only be applied in those cases where an inmate was able to convince another correctional officer to challenge the misconduct on their behalf. Even though everyone in the institution knew of this practice, the inmate's word alone was never viewed as sufficient to contest the alleged violation. Absent any corroborating testimony the inmate would be sent to the "hole." It is also important to note that the officer who actually submitted the bogus misconduct was never reprimanded for their actions.

Though the above accounts describe the unethical use of solitary confinement as a structural apparatus of institutional control, the use of isolated confinement becomes particularly egregious when used to control an inmate suffering from a serious mental illness. As a clinical intern, I witnessed the effects of such confinement first hand. What I found most clinically unethical was the institutional consequences imposed on a mentally ill client who could not tolerate the severe conditions of disciplinary custody. In the following chapters I will explore the phenomenology of solitary confinement more thoroughly; however, I would like to briefly explore an aspect of this type of confinement that is not often addressed: How do the conditions of solitary confinement help to evoke individual behavior that results in the extension of time in disciplinary custody?

For most individuals who are placed in solitary confinement for having violated penitentiary rules, the sentence is served and they are returned to general population. For the mentally ill individual who is suddenly placed in solitary confinement, one of the most daunting challenges they will face is their ability to successfully serve their allotted time in segregated custody. The mentally ill inmate, then, is faced with two different challenges: (1) Can they tolerate the conditions of their sentence, regardless its duration, without becoming overwhelmed by symptoms related to their condition? (2) Can they serve their sentence without incurring more disciplinary time? Though both of these concerns are interrelated, how the second question is answered is central to whether or not the mentally ill inmate's stay in solitary will be brief or indefinite.

On entering solitary confinement, the individual, regardless their current "psychological status," enters the same physical space as any other inmate: a small steel and concrete cell, stainless steel commode and sink, and a stainless steel bedframe with thin mattress. However, what is not the same is the phenomenology which unfolds for each. For the mentally ill individual, the sparse cell and lack of normal human interaction can become so intolerable that the inmate may simply lash out, either at themselves or someone else, accruing more disciplinary time in the process. As a result, it is not at all unusual to have an individual build up literally years of disciplinary custody time after being initially sentenced to just 30 days in the "hole."

What would generally be a "manageable" sentence for certain incarcerated individuals becomes almost unlivable for those suffering with chronic mental illness. Take, for example, the individual struggling with borderline personality disorder. For such an individual entering solitary confinement, a number of significant challenges must be addressed. Perhaps the most immediate of these challenges is the absence of intersubjective experience. Such an absence is particularly relevant here, because the very definition of the "borderline self" emerges from these experiences. Within the diminished environment of disciplinary custody these relationships are denied and the self is left to its own designs, which is simply incapable of filling this psychological void. One simply needs to identify the characteristics of this pathological style of relationality to recognize just how debilitating this experience can be for those suffering with this chronic disorder.

The Diagnostic and Statistical Manual of Mental Disorders defines borderline personality disorder (BPD) as "… a pervasive pattern of instability of interpersonal relationships, self-image and affects and marked impulsivity …" (APA, 2013, p. 325). BPD is further characterized by "frantic efforts to avoid real or imagined abandonment, relationships characterized by extremes of idealization and devaluation, identity disturbance, impulsivity, recurrent suicidal behavior or gestures, chronic feelings of emptiness and intense anger" (APA, 2013). When an individual, suffering from this condition is placed in solitary, these characteristics are intensified. In fact, the "acting out behavior," which is generally characteristic of this diagnostic category, is actually a desperate attempt to be in a relationship, albeit in a highly dysfunctional way. However, the increase of these symptoms almost always has the accompanying consequence of additional disciplinary sanctions. An example will be helpful to illuminate this point.

One of my clients, whom I will call F, was serving a relatively short sentence for a drug conviction. He had been able to remain in general population for approximately two years, but ultimately was sent to solitary confinement for violation of penitentiary rules. Diagnosed with BPD, it became immediately clear that he would be unable to tolerate the conditions of disciplinary custody. Within a rather short period of time, he accumulated nearly 10 years of misconduct time, which would need to be served in its entirety before he could be returned to general population. However, given that his disciplinary time exceeded the duration of his maximum sentence, he would be required to not only "max out" that sentence, but serve nearly all of that time in disciplinary custody. In fact, his behavior was so uncontrollable while held in solitary confinement that he was often transferred to different penitentiaries in the system, when current facilities were no longer able or willing to control his explosive behavior.

The context of segregated custody powerfully evoked the whole range of borderline functioning in this individual, which was evidenced by daily bouts of uncontrollable anger, intense feelings of abandonment, and various episodes of self-harm. Though I was able to have him taken from his cell on a regular basis to meet with him individually, the conditions were so overwhelming for someone with his diagnosis that it is difficult to claim that any legitimate benefit could be achieved. I would regularly discuss F's case with my supervisor, who agreed that it was unethical to allow this situation to continue. We needed to try something new. When we approached prison administrators about perhaps finding a way to decrease his overall disciplinary time, they immediately rejected the idea, voicing their concern that such special treatment could have a "contagion effect" on the institution.

Regardless the position of prison administrators, there would simply be no legitimate way to address these borderline symptoms if F was going to continue to be housed in solitary. Furthermore, they seemed unable to recognize that most of F's behavioral difficulties were the direct result of his placement in disciplinary custody. Though they certainly wanted something to be done about the constant difficulties this individual was creating, they were completely unwilling to change any of the circumstances that were clearly contributing to the problem. The fact that he had literally years left to serve of his disciplinary custody time precluded any possible return to general population. As a result, the behavior continued and the non-clinical staff involved with the segregated housing unit became more and more overwhelmed with a situation that seemed likely to go on indefinitely. As this situation persisted, everyone involved could at least agree on one thing: The situation would only get worse if this individual was going to remain in disciplinary custody.

The clinical supervisor for the penitentiary used this fact to once again try to persuade prison administrators to allow him to structure a program that would allow F to be removed from solitary confinement and allow him the opportunity to earn his way back to general population. The administrators appeared to agree and the plan was put into place. As a result, F was immediately moved to the mental health unit and given a cell that was located away from the other individuals on that ward. Though he was still isolated, he was not in solitary and was therefore no longer required to be cuffed when he was outside of the cell. The premise of the plan was simple: Remove F from the overwhelming conditions of traditional disciplinary custody and reward good behavior with minor amenities and regularly cut time from his existing misconduct record. However, though the plan presumably was approved by penitentiary officials, after a month or so, the program fell apart due to a verbal altercation between a correctional officer and F, resulting in his return to disciplinary custody.

Though it would perhaps be "reasonable" to surmise that the failure of this program was largely due to F and his inability to control his behavior, this was not the case. Rather, the program failed for the simple reason that the correctional officers involved with his daily supervision did not agree that this individual should be afforded any special privileges and actually thought he should be returned to the segregated housing unit. There were numerous examples of the officers failing to honor the agreed rewards for good behavior, which of course resulted in F becoming agitated and verbally aggressive. These obvious attempts at disrupting the program were brought to the attention of the Security Deputy who did nothing. F was returned to solitary confinement with the expected results.

What these three accounts reveal is the various ways in which the practice of solitary confinement may be unethically employed to satisfy the utilitarian strategies of a specific penitentiary system. Central to this utilitarian process is a utility of rationalized retribution, which seeks to pursue an "ends justifies the means" attitude by which institutional harm may be justified and pursued as a "legitimate" strategy of control. So prominent is this philosophical perspective that it is often intentionally employed to circumvent existing penitentiary practice so as to achieve a specific end.

With the first account, an individual was placed immediately into solitary confinement even though this act specifically violates penitentiary regulations. Seemingly aware of this fact, facility administrators constructed a bogus scenario, which was then used to justify this illegitimate practice. When confronted about the veracity of these "facts" nothing was done. In the second account, penitentiary culture had normalized a process by which correctional officers may prevent individuals from being legitimately paroled from prison and in the third account, a mentally ill individual was forced to languish in solitary confinement with horrific results, all in the name of control.

Within this context, the pursuit of institutional control, which is often employed within the "logic" of such practices, takes on a much more nefarious connotation, which seems far removed from a purely utilitarian point of view. Though these "uses" of solitary confinement are ostensibly rationalized from a perspective of institutional control and security, they are informed by a utility of rational retribution that allows for their application within a variety of correctional contexts. As a result, the institutionally mandated function and purpose of solitary confinement – disciplinary segregation for the violation of penitentiary rules or to ensure the safety of a given inmate – is now expanded or extended to include these other "examples," regardless their legality.

When situated within such a rationalized structure, all retribution is deemed legitimate as long as it adheres to certain normative parameters concerning its actual application and use. As such, this recognized utility is often allowed to circumvent existing penitentiary practice when conceptualized for the purpose of satisfying some accepted or "rationalized" result. What these situations reveal is the willingness to blur legal and institutional practices in the name of this utility of retribution and the "correctional results" they provide. These examples also reflect what Agamben has described as the *state of exception*.

Agamben (2005/2003) has described the state of exception as a zone of indifference, which emerges from the blurring of the recognized lines of legal and political demarcation. Included within this concept is the "recognition" that certain individuals or groups cannot be "accommodated" within the existing political or institutional system, requiring, therefore, that another course of "action" be taken (this concept will be more thoroughly explored in Chapter three). Within the context of penitentiary practice generally, and solitary confinement specifically, the state of exception emerges as a result of the process of rationalized retribution. As a "practical function" of this process, solitary confinement comes to symbolize the locality where this state of exception is manifested.

As can be witnessed in the above accounts, the use of solitary confinement is appropriated to accommodate its "expanded" function as the apparatus of this state of exception. Though it retains it's more traditional function as a strategy of penitentiary control, within these contexts or spatialities it is transformed into a zone of indifference, which extends the "utility" of this practice. As a result, the traditional rules and regulations that normally govern the practice of solitary confinement become suspended within this emerging zone of indifference (de la Durantaye, 2009, p. 336). An example of this process can be clearly witnessed with the creation and use of the military prison located at Guantanamo Bay, Cuba.

In the aftermath of the terrifying success of the 9/11 attacks, which targeted the World Trade Center in Manhattan and the Pentagon in Northern Virginia, the War on Terror was born. Central to this strategy was the declaration made by then President George W. Bush, who stated that any noncitizen of the United States could be held indefinitely and without specific charge if suspected of some involvement in terrorist activities (Arrigo & Bersot, 2014; Ek, 2006; Gregory, 2006; Lanier, Polizzi, & Wade, 2014). However, this proclamation was not without its difficulties. The most glaringly obvious constitutional challenge to such a strategy was that it would be illegal to detain someone without formal charge and hold that individual indefinitely within the legal jurisdiction of the United States. In an attempt to circumvent the constitutional protections enjoyed by defendants in US courts, the prison facility located at Guantanamo Bay, Cuba was constructed.

The initial rationale for the construction and use of the military prison at Guantanamo Bay was to provide a facility that could be utilized to incarcerate those individuals identified by the US government as believed to be involved in terrorist activities or organizations. Included here, of course, was the "ancillary" benefit, which provided "sufficient distance" from the legal protections provided by the US Constitution. In exploring the initial rationale offered by the logic of the War on Terror, Agamben (2005/2003) offered a powerful observation:

What is new about President Bush's order is that it radically erases any legal status of the individual, thus producing a legally unnamable and unclassifiable being. Not only do the Taliban captured in Afghanistan not enjoy the state of POWs as defined by the Geneva Convention, they do not even have the status of prisoners charged with a crime according to American laws (p. 3).

What becomes most germane to this current formulation of solitary confinement as a state of exception is that it identifies a "class" of human beings, who "… for some reason cannot be integrated into the political system" (Agamben, 2005/2003, p. 2). As was witnessed in the above accounts, solitary confinement becomes the identified locality for those individuals who cannot be "appropriately controlled" within the "normal" function of the penitentiary system. Once so identified by the utility of rationalized retribution, the line of demarcation between the legal applications of this form of institutionalized control becomes blurred by the institutional necessity this process seems to evoke.

The changing landscape of segregated confinement: a very brief developmental history

Since the very inception of the penitentiary system in America, the practice of solitary confinement has been used as a central strategy by which to control and subjugate its inmate populations. Employed initially as an "experimental" strategy of rehabilitation, it was believed that the experience of total isolation would evoke in the individual the ability to reflect on their past deeds and create the opportunity for contrition and redemption (Arrigo & Trull, 2015; Guenther, 2013; Rothman, 2002; Sellin, 1970; Shalev, 2011; Smith, 2004; Suedfeld & Roy, 1975; Toch, 2003). So "promising" were the correctional expectations of such a strategy that they became commonplace in penitentiary systems across the United States and Europe, beginning in the 1820s through the 1860s. However, by the later 1800s (Rovner, 2016; Smith, 2008; Toch, 2003), the practice of solitary confinement had lost a great deal of its correctional favor as a rehabilitation strategy and was now employed almost exclusively as a strategy of punishment reserved for the most difficult inmates or as a protective strategy for those individuals deemed to be vulnerable in the general population environment of a given institution (Shalev, 2011).

Fast-forwarding to the current correctional context, solitary confinement continues to be used as a general strategy by which to isolate those inmates who have violated institutional rules, or who have been deemed a threat to the security of the facility; it has also been employed as a protective strategy for those inmates whose safety would be compromised if they remained in general population. Concomitant with this more traditional reliance on solitary confinement has been the increasing proliferation of supermax facilities within the United States and elsewhere. As a result, the practice of segregated confinement, traditionally reserved for those placed in disciplinary custody, has been expanded to reflect a strategy of confinement employed by entire institutions. Though these two types of confinement are technically different aspects of correctional practice, they do share a very similar attitude, which differs only in degree, but not in kind. As a result, the ethically challenged practice of solitary confinement not only continues, but has become more prevalent as a legitimate strategy of correctional control.

The most obvious question which comes to mind is how we have got to this moment in correctional praxis such that we are now returning to a philosophy of confinement that has been clearly shown to provide very little rehabilitative benefit. One answer to this question seems to be related to the practice of mass incarceration, which began in the early 1980s in the United States. As incarceration rates began their meteoric rise, largely fueled by the "War on Drugs," different strategies of incarceration were required to address the drastically overcrowded conditions of the US penitentiary system (Lanier, Polizzi & Wade, 2014).

"Lockdown facilities" as they are euphemistically called, became an "easy fix" to the solution of inmate overcrowding and the multiplicity of problems this practice evoked. Within this new and expanded application of isolated confinement, inmates are often required to spend most of their time in their cell, with fewer opportunities for more traditional types of interaction with staff or other inmates. As increasing prison populations overwhelmed the limited resources of the correctional system, this strategy has come to be seen as an effective way of addressing this issue. However, what are the ethical considerations and implications for such a strategy of control?

What has remained equally true, regardless the intent of those individuals and institutions who have employed this penal strategy over the course of its history, is the profound psychological assault such an experience may inflict on those who are so targeted for this manner of correctional intervention; this observation is particularly germane for those individuals held in solitary confinement for a prolonged period of time (Haney, 2003, 2008, 2009, 2012; Haney, Weill, Bakhshay & Lockett, 2016; O'Keefe, 2007). Whether employed as a strategy of rehabilitation, as it was originally intended, or as a punitive strategy of control, the psychological implications evoked by the use of solitary confinement are undeniable, and have been well documented since its inception (Haney, 2003, 2008; Smith, 2008; Toch, 2003). One of the central features of this penal strategy is witnessed in its specific intent to socially isolate the individual, which results in the total disruption of the very ontological foundation of human experience (Guenther, 2013; Suedfeld & Roy, 1975; Toch, 2003).

Toward a phenomenology of solitary confinement

Viewed from a phenomenological perspective, the experience of solitary confinement, regardless its specific institutional specifications, denies or severely limits the very possibility of human relationality and embodiment, which in turn can greatly transform one's relationship to self. Absent the presence or possibility of regular social interaction with other individuals, the experience of self must resort to a desperate attempt to re-establish some manner of relationality that is potentially capable of addressing this extreme and often indeterminate episode of isolation (Haney, 2003, 2012; O'Donnell, 2014). Though certain individuals have been able to manifest a sufficient degree of psychological resolve to survive this experience, others of course have not been so lucky (Goffman, 1961; Rubin, 2015).

Central to this phenomenology – which will be thoroughly explored in Chapters four and five – is the relationship between the body and world, which is specifically configured by the structural fact of solitary confinement. At its most general, human embodiment finds itself situated within a world that invites a range of corporeal motility and relationality within various manifestations of spatial possibility. The very experience of embodied subjectivity becomes meaningful through my ability to take up in a co-constituting way my relationships with others and my experience of the physical world (Merleau-Ponty, 1945/2012). Within each of these manifestations of bodily engagement emerges a configuration of spatiality relative to a specific experience that is configured by the possibilities of perceptual motility and distance (Barbaras, 1999/2006). Regardless how these experiences are perceived – be it by some type of affective stance or by some manifestation of physical space – a distance emerges from the in-between of these encounters and helps to construct their meaning predicated on the potentiality of this *living movement*.

In his text, *Desire and Distance: Introduction to a Phenomenology of Perception*, Renaud Barbaras (1999/2006) makes the following observation:

> One has no choice but to concede that bodies that perceive are *living* bodies and that they are distinguished from other corporeal beings (moreover, but to a lesser degree, from the largely immobile living beings that are plants) by their capacity for movement. It is therefore on the level of this constitutive motility of the living being that we must be able to access the ultimate meaning of subjectivity, it is a subject capable of movement that the perceiving subject can be grasped in its true being (p. 86).

From this perspective, the living body or the living-in-being, is predicated on not merely the corporal body, but the body which is capable of motility. Barbaras extends Merleau-Ponty's observation concerning the philosophical status of the body by theorizing that to configure the body as a theory of perception requires that it be situated within this potentiality for movement. "Beings capable of moving are the very ones capable of feeling; feeling and moving are the two aspects of the same mode of living, because movement assumes the desire for a goal, which itself requires the capacity for perceiving it" (Barbaras, 1999/2006, p. 87). The observation provided by Barbaras is of particular use when it is applied to the context of the phenomenology of solitary confinement.

Within this context, the very possibility of movement is drastically restricted, which ultimately disrupts the affective and motile aspects of human embodiment and perception. If the foundation of human perception is predicated on motility, if subjectivity is configured by a body capable of movement, then the practice and structure of solitary confinement evokes a state of exception that is geared toward disrupting the ontological ground of human existence. However, it is important to recognize that motility within this context is not merely a mechanical aspect of embodied subjectivity, but the very ontological quality that makes the full range of human perception possible. Barbaras (1999/2006) concludes that the very possibility of the subject is based on the possibility of what he identifies as the "autonomy of living movement, this capacity of continually recreating one's self" (p. 93). The structure of solitary confinement precludes such autonomy.

What will follow?

In Chapter two I will explore the historical development of the use of solitary confinement, and follow its various "functional" transformations within the American prison system from its introduction in the early 1820s to its more contemporary iterations. Included in this developmental history will be discussion concerning the emergence of the supermax penitentiary, which was first introduced within the United States in the early 1930s with the opening of Alcatraz prison, up to the contemporary use of these total confinement facilities.

In Chapter three a philosophical analysis will be provided concerning the historical development of solitary confinement, which will include the more recent manifestation of the supermax prison. Even though the function and purpose of solitary confinement is categorically different from that of the supermax penitentiary, the underlying "logic" of both are basically philosophically the same. The main focus of this discussion, then, will be to explore the various ways in which the physical construction and structure of these spaces reveals a specific philosophical orientation, which in turn elicits a very specific intentionality toward those intended for this manner of incarceration. As a result, solitary confinement and the supermax facility will be explored from the perspective that each constructs a specifically configured locality wherein the state of exception may reside.

Chapter four will explore the phenomenology of this experience from the perspective of Merleau-Ponty's conceptualization of embodied subjectivity and Barbaras' notion of living being. The chapter will begin with a theoretical discussion of the philosophical contours of embodied subjectivity, and its possible significance relative to the practice of solitary confinement, as this relates to its more traditional application, as well as its use within supermax penitentiaries. Included in this discussion will be actual accounts from individuals who have either experienced the isolation of solitary confinement or who have been incarcerated in supermax facilities. Central to this discussion will be how the physical space of solitary confinement or supermax incarceration confronts the ontological realities of embodied subjectivity, particularly as this relates to the ontology of movement, as well as the various strategies employed to lessen the most onerous aspects of this experience.

2

A VERY BRIEF HISTORY OF SOLITARY CONFINEMENT AND THE SUPERMAX PENITENTIARY

The practice of solitary confinement was a core component of the new penitentiary system emerging in America in the early 1800s. Central to this correctional strategy was the belief that isolation from the world, and its sinful ways, would be the essential ingredient of the rehabilitative process. It was believed that if the individual was sufficiently isolated and left to the power of their own reflection and contemplation, they would recognize the error of their ways and, as a result, would refrain from any subsequent criminal behavior on their release from the penitentiary.

Ironically enough, the practice of solitary confinement was initially intended as a necessary replacement for the squalid conditions of jails commonly employed in the late eighteenth and early nineteenth centuries (O'Donnell, 2014; Rothman, 2002; Scull, 2006). These institutions were often overcrowded, understaffed, and lacking in the most basic resources necessary to humanely address the material and psychological needs of the occupants whom they housed. The cramped quarters and unhygienic conditions often became a breeding ground for a variety of contagious diseases, which often made placement in such institutions literally fatal. Needless to say, the rehabilitative intent of such correctional confinement was rarely ever achieved. "Prisons were seen as incubators of a kind of disease that, unchecked, might act to deplete the community of God-fearing and law-abiding citizens who came into contact with prisoners, but also of a kind of vice that served to swell the ranks of the criminal classes (O'Donnell, 2014, p. 3).

In an attempt to respond to the contagion threat posed by the existing system of incarceration, reformers began to explore a strategy that could provide some protection to the social order relative to the contagion threat posed by criminality along with some legitimate hope for what Howard identified as a "moral reclamation" of the offending individual (O'Donnell, 2014). However, such a strategy would require that the very structure and praxis of such facilities be rethought.

Though the fact of incarceration was able to address the immediate challenge confronting the prison reform movement – that was, the isolation of the criminal from the "normalcy" of law-abiding social life – it would also need to address the obvious contagion threat that currently existed within the walls of the penitentiary. The incarceration of the offending individual would simply not be sufficient if the desired result of moral reclamation was to be realized. Given that the environmental conditions of these facilities were conducive to the spread of contagious disease and physical and psychological predation, a different strategy would need to be employed to address the day-to-day realities of correctional confinement. The practice of solitary confinement become viewed as the answer to this question.

The emerging penitentiary system in America therefore reflected a new type of transformative correctional space that merged the pentitive aspects of the confessional with the secular theology of Enlightenment rationality (Foucault, 1977/1995; Rothman, 2002; Smith, 2004; Weber, 1978) In explaining this idea further, Smith (2004) observes that "From this perspective, rationality does not in itself constitute a normative foundation that can replace moral, value-laden considerations arising from, for example, religious convictions. 'Rationality' refers to a mode of conduct rather than a substantive set of values" (p. 196). The manifestation of this newly emerging repentant rationality was incorporated into the first American penitentiaries located in Philadelphia, Pennsylvania and Auburn, New York. Though slightly different in strategy and scope, each of these institutions sought to apply the practice of social isolation as the process by which a non-criminal version of the self would be fabricated. Though the strategy of social isolation was viewed as the central core of the rehabilitative process, slight differences in approach did exist.

With the Auburn model, inmates were allowed to interact with other inmates, but were required to do so in complete silence; whereas under the Pennsylvania model, inmates were completely isolated and were required to perform nearly all penitentiary tasks in their cell with very little interaction with other human beings. The lack of social interaction and the hours spent in solitary confinement were intended to turn the thoughts of the incarcerated individual away from the temptations of the secular world. As a result, it was further rationalized that such an experience would direct the individual inward and cause them to focus on their relationship to God and awaken in them the need to repent (Arrigo & Trull, 2015; Rothman, 2002; Smith, 2008).

So popular was this new idea of correctional transformation that it soon made its way to Europe. Though the Auburn model was viewed with more favor by the newly emerging correctional institutions of Europe, the Pennsylvania model also had its adherents. However, by the late 1840s in America, it was starting to become evident that the application of solitary confinement imposed a high psychological price on those who were forced to endure this correctional practice. In a report written in 1845 by Thomas Cleveland, the acting head of the prison of Rhode Island, the following observation was made concerning the psychological impact of solitary confinement:

Persons who have never been deprived even of a small portion of what may be called their *normal stimulus*, for any considerable length of time, are little aware of its salutary and indispensable influence … The succession of day and night, the changing seasons through which we are constantly passing, are all in continual action upon the springs of life. The momentary and ever-changing objects which present themselves to the eye, the continual and rapid variety of sounds which present themselves to the ear, and, in short, the perpetual succession of phenomena, which addresses themselves to the senses, are all, in a state of personal liberty, and except in the periodical intermissions of sleep, constantly operating upon the brain, and supplying it with that normal stimulus so necessary to the production of moral, physical, and intellectual health (Cleveland quoted in Toch, 2003, p. 223).

By beginning as he does, Cleveland powerfully established the comparative difference or phenomenology between normal experience and the experience of solitary confinement. In his report, Cleveland highlighted how the most fundamental aspects of taken-for-granted human experience become drastically disrupted by a practice that was initially recognized for its positive rehabilitative influence. He continues by stating:

Now, suddenly abstract from a man these influences, to which he has been so keen accustomed; shut him up with but scanty resources of his own to keep the powers of the mind in action, in a solitary cell, where he must pass the same unvarying round, from week to week, with hope depressed, with no subjects for reflection but those give him pain to review, in the scenes of his former life; after a few days, with no new impressions made upon his senses ... one unvarying sameness relaxes the attention and concentration of the mind, and it will not be thought strange, that, though the consequent debility and irritability of its organ, the mind should wander and become impaired ... (Cleveland quoted in Toch, 2003, p. 223).

Cleveland's observations, which emerged from his clinical experience working with these individuals at the Rhode Island prison, were able to establish the relationship between solitary confinement and its psychological effects on the inmate population. Similar results were also being reported at a number of correctional institutions both in America and Europe (Smith, 2008), which within a 30-year time frame saw a drastic decrease in the regular use of this type of correctional practice. Though the use of solitary confinement continued to be employed as a strategy of correctional intervention after this period, in spite of all of the known psychological implications, its use became almost exclusively employed as a punitive response to control difficult inmates who were either unable or unwilling to conform to penitentiary rules.

The transitional movement away from the use of solitary confinement as a central strategy of rehabilitative change, precipitated by the adverse psychological effects it visited on inmate populations, ironically enough did not provide sufficient reason to discontinue its use. Rather, what we witness in the historical "evolution" of this practice is the emergence of a different type of rational legitimacy, which simply replaced its former theological emphasis with a utility of rationalized retribution. Gone from this practice was any connection to its repentant rehabilitative past. Though viewed as a failure relative to its ability to evoke individual contrition and transformation, it was now seen as a powerful tool of correctional intervention by which to impose a regime of disciplinary control on those inmates who failed to comply with penitentiary rules (Goffman, 1961).

The contemporary context of solitary confinement

As was stated above, the current use of solitary confinement has been employed as a punitive strategy by which to control incarcerated populations. Though no longer viewed as a core component of the rehabilitative process, it continues to be utilized as a strategy of correctional control. Whether employed as a function of penitentiary disciplinary strategy or more generally employed within the confines of the supermax penitentiary, solitary confinement and its use continues unabated, in spite of its well-documented effects on inmate populations (Arrigo & Milovanovic, 2009; Arrigo, Bersot & Sellers, 2011; Guenther, 2013; Haney, 2008, 2016; Kupers, 2014, 2016; Mears & Reisig, 2006; O'Donnell, 2014; Pizarro & Narag, 2008; Smith, 2008, Toch, 2003).

As a tool of correctional intervention within a given institution, solitary confinement is generally employed in two ways: as a disciplinary strategy of control or as a protective strategy of isolation, used to either protect a certain individual from some type of danger within the penitentiary or to isolate an inmate viewed as a potential threat to penitentiary security, in the absence of any specific infraction that would require such a disciplinary sanction (Arrigo, Bersot, & Sellers, 2011; Riveland, 1999). However, as Arrigo, Bersot, & Sellers observe, "Although solitary confinement facilities are designed to physically isolate and constructively curtail the violent behavior of disruptive inmates, there are variations in the types and length of imprisonment" (p. 62). Based on this observation, it should not be surprising that the use of solitary confinement as a strategy of control is most often employed in those institutions generally classified as maximum security facilities by a given correctional system. This is not to say that solitary confinement is absent from those institutions that are classified at a lesser level of security; rather, it merely reflects the reality that this type of punitive correctional practice is less frequently employed at such facilities – a fact that is often evidenced by the limited number of cells available for this type of disciplinary segregation in these lower-classified institutions. "The kind of control exercised in these maximum security settings is technologically sophisticated and planned down to the smallest detail. The myriad elements of housing design, placement, and daily routine shaping these prisoners' situations rest on the assumption that rational practices underlie the operation of 'the system'" (Rhodes, 2004, p. 5).

The advent of the supermax penitentiary

Though the use of solitary confinement has been a part of American penal strategy since its inception, the growing popularity of the supermax penitentiary is a relatively new phenomenon. This type of correctional strategy was initially employed at the federal prison developed on Alcatraz Island, located in San Francisco Bay in 1934 (Ward & Werlich, 2003). The driving rationale of this new federal correctional facility was to house a relatively small number of infamous American criminals in a high-security institution. However, as Ward & Werlich (2003) observe, the functional purpose of Alcatraz was not to simply provide a stricter disciplinary regime for the most disruptive inmates in the federal system. Rather, they argue, "The nation's first super maximum security prison was primarily intended to represent a powerful symbol of the consequences for serious criminal conduct, not to control prison troublemakers" (p. 55).

As a result, the emergence of Alcatraz came to represent another manifestation of the rational utility of retribution discussed above. Up until this point, disciplinary isolation was used as a means to a specific correctional end; however, with the introduction of Alcatraz, disciplinary isolation became an end in itself and was employed as a strategy to address the general threat of serious criminal behavior. As a result, Alcatraz also became a reinforcing symbol, which supported the idea that "crime doesn't pay."

In this newest iteration of solitary confinement, all pretenses to rehabilitative transformation were stripped away, leaving only this naked utility of retribution and the correctional practices that it evoked. As a result, the day-to-day function and purpose of Alcatraz was to punish. Though the opportunity to work was allowed, if earned by the inmate, all other programmatic rehabilitative trappings where simply not available at this facility. "Alcatraz, which began operations in 1934, was established for the purposes of punishment, incarceration, and deterrence; there was no pretense that its 'habitual, intractable' prisoners could or would be 'rehabilitated'. It was to be a super prison for the super criminals caught by super cops" (Ward & Werlich, 2003, p. 55).

Ironically enough, Alcatraz still retained multiple levels of disciplinary custody that simply intensified the experience of social deprivation and isolation. Though the general day-to-day function of the institution greatly restricted the possibilities for regular social interaction, those inmates who attempted to escape or were violent toward either staff or other inmates were placed in special disciplinary segregation units that resulted in their total isolation from the outside world (Ward & Werlich, 2003) However, by the 1950s, critics had once again decried the use of such barbaric methods of correctional isolation and had begun to question once again the effectiveness of such strategies (Richards, 2008). "Incarceration under conditions of such severe separation from free society combined with so many deprivations was regarded as not only outdated, but counterproductive when compared to incentives for good 'conduct'" (Ward & Werlich, 2003). As a result, Alcatraz was finally closed in 1963, and was now viewed as a relic of a penal philosophy of a bygone era. Three months after the closing of Alcatraz, the Federal Bureau of Prisons opened a new facility in Marion, Illinois, which was touted to reflect a new era in correctional philosophy.

At the time that Alcatraz was decommissioned, most of the individuals held at that facility were transferred to other maximum security institutions within the federal system (Richards, 2008). Those inmates not sent elsewhere were to be housed at the new federal penitentiary located in Marion, Illinois. Similar in size to Alcatraz, USP Marion was designed to hold "… the 'incorrigibles,' or 'two percenters,' troublemakers who resisted prison authority or assaulted staff or other prisoners" (Richards, 2008, p. 9). However, unlike Alcatraz, Marion was envisioned to usher in a new chapter in American penal philosophy, which would be more clearly focused on the rehabilitative process and provide an alternative vision from correctional practices of the past.

Initially, USP Marion sought to fulfill this new possibility for correctional practice, which was evidenced by the availability of a variety of correctional programming and trained psychological staff dedicated to achieving this rehabilitative promise (Newbold, 2015). As a result, Marion quickly became the "correctional destination" for the most problematic inmates in both the federal and state systems. However, in a span of just 10 short years, the rehabilitative mood of this institution started to reflect a decided change.

In 1973 the first inmate control unit was introduced at Marion, which was used to isolate problem inmates from the rest of the prison population. By 1979 Marion had been designated as a Level 6 institution, which further limited prisoner movement. In the aftermath of a bloody six-day period of violence in 1983, during which two penitentiary officers and one inmate were killed, Marion became a total lockdown facility, which resulted in inmates being held in their cells 23 hours a day (Richards, 2008). By the mid-1980s, USP Marion had become a harsher example of the type of correctional facility it was originally designed to replace.

Rather than evolving into a representation of this new penal philosophy based on the potential of rehabilitative transformation, it came to be employed as an institution commissioned to house the most difficult prisoners in the federal system and ultimately marked the return of the utility of rationalized retribution. Though the history of solitary confinement as a strategy of isolated control has been discredited over the course of that same period of time that fact has not prevented its continued use and popularity as a method of correctional intervention. One could perhaps surmise that such a history would preclude its continued use, but that conclusion has not materialized. In fact, there has been a proliferation of such facilities in spite of this rather dubious history (Haney, 2009; Kupers, 2014; Mears & Reisig, 2006; Richards, 2015).

Currently, virtually every state DOC in the United States has some manner of supermax capability, as either a standalone facility or as a specifically designated unit within a lager correctional institution; this includes the Administrative Maximum Facility run by the Federal Bureau of Prisons located in Florence, CO., which houses the country's most notorious criminal population, both foreign and domestic (Binelli, 2015; Dey, 2015; Immarigeon, 2015; Taylor, 2015). Symbolic of the new Alcatraz, this federal supermax facility in many ways has incorporated much of the same "logic" which its predecessor sought to evoke, albeit with a greater sense of architectural and technological flare.

Much like the initial intent of Alcatraz, the current generation of supermax facilities have become "… an extreme variant of solitary confinement" (Shalev, 2011, p. 155). However, unlike the more "traditional" use of this type of correctional practice, these new facilities reflect a different manifestation of the criminal justice machine, which has become predicated on the utility of rationalized retribution, whose first and perhaps only operational purpose is to provide an environment of control and deprivation and punishment. Shalev (2011) seems to substantiate this point by observing "These prisons were built as an addition to, not a replacement of, existing segregation units that one would find in most prisons and jails, thus dramatically increasing the number of solitary confinement cells throughout the United States" (p. 153).

However, this strategy does not simply create a greater capacity for the use of solitary confinement; rather, it reflects a fundamental transformation of this institutional space, which now seeks to punish the act of crime as a social event with immediate isolation prior to any of the formerly required violations of correctional rules or regulations. For those individuals housed in such facilities, a double penalty is imposed: the loss of liberty as well as the loss of normal human contact. The loss of liberty is imposed due to the individual's criminal conviction, whereas the use of isolation is employed to punish the very existence of the perpetrator of the criminal act.

The process of this "double utility" reflects more than simply the legally sanctioned punishment for the violation of criminal law. Included here is a type of correctional intervention that strikes at the very ontological foundation of human experience. For example, if it was reported that a person in the community was guilty of holding an individual or group of individuals in a setting more or less similar to that used to house individuals in solitary or supermax confinement, the public would be shocked. They would almost certainly empathize with those held under such inhumane conditions and would likely view the perpetrator as either evil or psychopathic. Yet the same type of concern seems far less likely for those held in these very restrictive correctional settings.

Perhaps an immediate response to such a comparison would observe that the individual held in the community was a victim of a crime, and therefore cannot be legitimately compared with a lawbreaker receiving a legitimate legal sanction. Though this aspect of the argument would certainly be correct, it would not address the extreme conditions that the offender would experience on their incarceration. The legitimate punishment for certain crimes is incarceration. However, that fact cannot be used to also legitimize a manner of incarceration which extends the rationale of punishment to a psychopathic degree.

Rather than reflecting a legitimate criminal sanction for illegal behavior, the continued use of solitary confinement and the growing use of supermax penitentiaries have come to exemplify what Agamben has described as the state of exception. As a state of exception solitary confinement and supermax incarceration become zones of indifference whereby this practice is legitimated by the legal process in the name of political expediency. This idea will be pursued within the developmental history of this type of correctional practice, as well as within the context provided by a number of Supreme Court opinions, which have refused to recognize that this type of state cruelty should be prohibited for its violation of Eighth Amendment protections against cruel and unusual punishment.

THE DEVELOPMENTAL HISTORY OF SOLITARY AND SUPERMAX CONFINEMENT: TOWARD A PHENOMENOLOGY OF THE STATE OF EXCEPTION

In the previous chapter, a very brief developmental history was provided concerning solitary confinement, which was followed by a brief discussion of the emergence of supermax penitentiaries beginning with the opening of Alcatraz in 1933. In this chapter a more philosophically situated discussion will be offered concerning the ethical implications concerning the structural realities imposed on those individuals placed in such a restrictive correctional setting. Central to this discussion will be an exploration of the shifting intentionally, which was often used to justify the phenomenology of this type of correctional intervention. It will be further argued that the apparatus of solitary confinement is the process by which this state exception reveals itself as a zone of indifference, ultimately resulting in the continued use of this extreme example of correctional practice. To better conceptualize this perspective, I would like to begin with an observation provided by Alasdair MacIntyre (1988) in his text, *Whose Justice? Which Rationality?*

In his attempt to rehabilitate Aristotle and Virtue Ethics for the contemporary reader, MacIntyre (1988) states "Aristotle's mistake, and the mistake of others who have reasoned similarly, was not to understand how domination of a certain kind is in fact the cause of those characteristics of the dominated which are then invoked to justify unjustified domination" (p. 105). Though it is important to add that MacIntyre's observation was specifically intended to address Aristotle's view of women and his position concerning slavery, it is equally true that this observation has very important implications for the current discussion. The relationship between dominator and the dominated can be easily recognized within the context of the practice of solitary confinement and the expanding use of isolated incarceration strategies currently employed by supermax penitentiaries.

As MacIntyre observes, unjustified domination normally occurs when a specific group is designated as being in some way ontologically inferior, which in turn is employed to rationalize what follows. Once in place, the structural realities of this form of domination are ignored relative to the injurious effects it imposes on those so dominated. Any attempt by the dominated individual or group to challenge the meaning or structure of these conditions is then used as the evidentiary basis by on which more stringent strategies of domination may be employed. When placed within the context of the work of Giorgio Agamben, this process reflects what he has identified as the state of exception.

Agamben (2005/2003) describes the state of exception as a type of "… no-man's land between public law and political fact, and between the juridical order and life …" (p. 1). As such, the normal confluence between legal and political "boundaries and authority" becomes blurred to the extent that this no-man's land is not only constructed but becomes legitimized as a functioning aspect of this legal-political structure He goes on to observe that the state of exception "… allows for the physical elimination of not only political adversaries but entire categories of citizens who for some reason cannot be integrated into the political system (p. 3). Initially emerging as a response to a perceived state of emergency – that is, the War on Drugs, the War on Terror, and the construction of the prison at Guantanamo Bay – this process then becomes more or less validated as a normal function of the apparatus of a given state.

Agamben (2005/2003) observes that the more traditional definition of the state of exception reflects a locality within or between the law and the political system, which manifests "… a (total or partial) suspension of the juridical order" (p. 23). However, he argues, "The simple topographical opposition (inside/outside) implicit in these theories seems insufficient to account for the phenomenon that it should explain" (p. 23). If the state of exception is a suspension of the juridical order, how can that dynamic be contained within that order and if it exists outside, unrelated to the law, how does it allow such a possibility to occur (Agamben, 2005/2003); de la Durantaye, 2009)? In an attempt to resolve this concern, Agamben (2005/2003) states that:

> In truth, the state of exception is neither external nor internal to the juridical order, and the problem of defining it concerns precisely a threshold, or zone of indifference, where inside and outside do not exclude each other but rather blur with each other. The suspension of the norm does not mean its abolition, and the zone of anomie that it establishes is not (or at least claims not to be) unrelated to the juridical order (p.23).

Central to this new configuration of the state of exception is this zone of indifference that is neither a total rejection of a particular normative practice nor unrelated to the juridical order that allows its existence (Agamben, 2005/2003; de la Durantaye, 2009; Gulli, 2007; Murray, 2010). Solitary confinement reflects both of these definitional characteristics: As a zone of indifference these practices establish a space where such dehumanizing isolation is not only permitted, but rationalized and legitimated by the courts in spite of the acknowledged harm these practices may impose on those so confined (Hartman, 2008). It is important to note that these zones of indifference often contain those individuals who cannot be otherwise incorporated into the existing political system; a strategy that seems to be also reflected in the proliferation of supermax units that are functionally structured to incapacitate rather than to rehabilitate the inmate populations under their control (Crewe, 2014).

The introduction of solitary confinement and the structural phenomenology that it evoked

The use of solitary confinement was initially introduced as an alternative strategy by which to address the squalid conditions of incarcerated existence in the America of the 1790s and beyond, while also enhancing the possibility of rehabilitative success. It was believed that if the inmate was sufficiently isolated from the distractions offered by the secular world, this would invite a more reflective environment by which to encourage a more repentant attitude in the individual. To achieve this result, the sparse environment of monastic life was to be employed as the core rehabilitative aspect of this newly emerging penitentiary system.

One of the first attempts at penitentiary reform took place at the Walnut Street prison located in Philadelphia in the late 1790s. Based on the twin pillars of strict discipline and individual transformation, a new prison experiment was begun. Central to this new penal philosophy was the blending of Enlightenment rationality with traditional religion, which, it was believed, would facilitate the total transformation of the individual (Smith, 2004). Unfortunately, the desired results of this "new" experiment never materialized and the consequences of this failure once again required that reformers pursue a different strategy.

To exemplify this change of direction in penal philosophy, the New York and Pennsylvania penitentiary systems were introduced. Unlike the previous iterations of prison reform, these models were to rely heavily on the physical and structural isolation of the inmate population, which would then be employed in the process of religious transformation.

> Solitary confinement played a major role in both prison systems on the rationale that corrupting influences were thereby rooted out and the discipline and rehabilitation of the prisoner made

possible. Isolation was also thought to be a formidable power that could promote the deterrent effect of punishment, thereby realizing the intended double purpose of the punishment: deterrence and rehabilitation (Smith, 2004, p. 205).

Within these various examples of the emerging penitentiary system in America, we witness a similar "concern" that is generally situated within the initial configuration of a state of exception: What to do with individuals who do not fit the structural expectations of a given social order? Initially, this question was answered by the simple fact of incarceration. However, due to the conditions this "solution" created, another strategy needed to be employed. Though the fact of incarceration "successfully" achieved the desired separation of the criminal element from law-abiding society, it was unable to achieve the same result within the actual walls of the institutions. The fact of extreme overcrowding, the presence of contagious disease and the ongoing physical threat to staff and other inmates, required that another strategy be employed. The introduction of solitary confinement seemed to satisfy both of these identified goals.

What justifies this initial manifestation of the penitentiary system as an example of a state of exception is witnessed in its attempt to transport the environment of monastic contemplation and prayer into the core strategy of correctional reform. The most obvious flaw in such a rehabilitative approach seems to be evidenced in the "decided" difference easily recognizable between monastic life and criminal incarceration. The individual entering such a religious experience normally does so voluntarily, with some degree of expectation concerning the challenges and demands such a spiritual journey will almost certainly impose. It seems difficult to believe that the same degree of expectation and intention would be equally present in those individuals who, after their criminal conviction, are confined to such a difficult environmental setting. In fact, these differing phenomenologies seem to be implied in Cleveland's powerful critique of this practice.

What is most relevant to the current discussion is the way in which the structural make-up of solitary confinement "deconstructs" the ontological relationality of human existence. Cleveland observed that "Persons who have never been deprived even of a small portion of what may be called their *normal stimulus*, for any considerable length of time, are little aware of its salutary and indispensable influence ..." (Cleveland quoted in Toch, 2003, p. 223). This indispensable influence which situates our relationality to world is the very thing that ties existence to its ontological "mooring." However, what seems most important for Cleveland are those taken-for-granted aspects of human experience that this type of incarceration denies: the experience of day moving to night, the ability to see, hear, or feel objects before us; those normal perceptual encounters with world on which this relational ontology is situated. In the absence of such experience, "the mind should wander and become impaired" (Cleveland quoted in Toch, 2003, p. 233).

Central to these competing phenomenologies – the perspective envisioned by the proponents of solitary confinement as rehabilitative strategy, and those speaking for individuals who were so confined – is the relationality this structure evokes. For the proponents of this approach, solitary confinement was intended to evoke the phenomenology of monastic transformation based on the desire to be forgiven by God for one's sins. Even when configured as a type of "monastic punishment," these conditions would be more likely to evoke a type of relationality that could draw one closer to God, and individual forgiveness. What seems most central to this result is a more or less voluntary engagement with a process which would configure the sparseness of such an experience in a decidedly different way.

For the incarcerated individual, a similar type of transformative phenomenology would be much more difficult to achieve for many of the reasons that Cleveland explains. The loss of the taken-for-granted perceptional aspects of normal everyday human experience would be denied in such a setting and, based on Cleveland's account, would not have been viewed as an invitation to get closer to God and repent for one's sinful ways, as the authors of this rehabilitative strategy had intended. Though such an experience could, for certain individuals, evoke the transformative phenomenology intended, it would likely only be possible after the initial period of perceptual disorientation had been overcome and reinvested with a religious intentionality.

If it is correct to say that the apparatus of solitary confinement was employed to cause a type of religious transformation, what does this instrumental causality reveal? In his text, *The Use of Bodies*, Agamben (2015) explores the relationship between causality and instrumentality in a way that is helpful to the current exploration of the structure of solitary confinement. He observes that:

> [w]hat defines the instrumental cause – for example, the axe in the hands of a carpenter who is making a bed – is the particularity of its action. On the one hand, it acts not in virtue of itself but in virtue of the principal agent (namely, the carpenter), but on the other hand, it works according to its own nature, which is that of cutting" (p. 70).

When placed within the context of the structure and causal intent of the initial manifestation of solitary confinement, the principal agent and the nature of this example can be clearly identified.

The particularity of the use of solitary confinement is recognized by its nature as that which isolates, punishes, and separates the individual from the world of normal experience. However, this nature can only be realized after its use has been configured by the principal agent, which in this example becomes the individual who believed that such an environment could "cause" a religious transformation of the incarcerated individual. Much like the axe, which needs the carpenter to fulfill the nature of both, the structure of solitary confinement needs the proponent of this type of rehabilitative process to realize its dual causality of punishment and religious transformation.

However, Agamben (2015) observes through his reading of Aquinas that the main focus of this dynamic should not be on the distinction between the principal agent and instrumental cause;

rather, it is more necessary to focus on "… the double action of the instrument …" (p. 71).

Aquinas (as quoted in Agamben, 2015) observes that an instrument "has a twofold action; one is instrumental, in respect of which it works not by its own power but by the power of the principal agent: the other is its proper action, which belongs to it in respect of its proper form …" (p. 71).

By configuring the instrument as a double action, it becomes that which it is and that which it is intended to cause by the power of the principal agent. The proper action of the instrument is only possible after the power of the principal agent has been also introduced. "Thus an instrument has two operations, one which belongs to it according to its own form, and another which belongs to it insofar as it is moved by the principal agent and which rises above the ability of its own form" (Agamben, 2015, p. 73). The configuration of the double action of the instrument is particularly recognizable within the context of solitary confinement.

From this perspective, the initial use of the instrument of the apparatus of solitary confinement – one which will be present in all other iterations of the same – also reflects this same double action. As an instrumental action, the physical space of solitary confinement reflects its proper form. However, with the introduction of the principal agent, this instrument is able to rise above its own form when employed in the name of punishment and religious transformation, while used in the service of the state, its principal agent. It is not until the proper form of solitary confinement is used by the principal agent that this instrumental action can be realized.

However, within a few decades after its introduction as the new strategy of rehabilitative change, the instrument of solitary confinement was removed from its religious intentionality and was now placed exclusively within the causal instrumentality of punishment. Though it's central function as an instrument of religious transformation had been totally rejected due to a rather dubious record of clinical effectiveness, such an observation of the facts did not preclude its continued use. With this change of function came a different instrumental causality, insofar as the intent of the principal agent was now exclusively articulated through the utility of rationalized retribution.

The inclusion, here, of Agamben's discussion of the instrument as provided by Aquinas, is intended to better situate the structural phenomenology that the physical space of solitary confinement evokes. From this perspective, the principal agent of this process is reflected within the utility of rationalized retribution, which transforms the proper form of the physical space of solitary confinement into an act of extreme punishment. It is important to recognize, however, that the proper form of solitary confinement is not fully manifest until it is "moved by the principal agent of rationalized retribution, which rises above the ability of its own form" (Agamben, 2015, p. 71).

Rationalized retribution and the introduction of the federal prisons at Alcatraz and Marion

After the transformation of solitary confinement into a solely punitive strategy of penitentiary control, it was not until this idea was "reintroduced" with the opening of the federal prison on Alcatraz Island in 1933 that this practice took on a different type instrumental causality. Prior to the opening of Alcatraz, most correctional institutions employed the use of disciplinary custody as a mechanism of inmate control. These institutions were generally configured with areas designated for general population, and those areas reserved for individuals deemed too dangerous for the less restrictive environment of the prison yard or cell block. However, with the introduction of Alcatraz, a more hybrid version of solitary confinement was launched that seemed to extend the practice of isolated lockup into the more general structure of the day-to-day running of the institution. Unlike the existing penitentiaries of the day, Alcatraz was specifically employed to confine society's most notorious criminals. As such, the mission of Alcatraz not only ushered in the age of supermax confinement, but was also used to represent "… a powerful symbol of the consequences for serious criminal conduct" (Ward & Werlich, 2003, p. 55) and not merely as an institution for difficult inmates.

The symbolic intent of Alcatraz – a super prison to hold the most publically notorious gangsters of the day – evoked the state of exception, which was now exclusively focused on the premise of punishment within this newly emerging utility of rationalized retribution. The publicity garnered by such "super criminals" as John Dillinger, Al Capone, Machine Gun Kelly, and others had so captured the public's imagination that it required an equally powerful response by law enforcement. Though certainly criminal, these individuals seemed to also reflect, for some, a type of heroic figure that was violently engaged with a corrupt and oppressive system (Kooistra, 1989). Not only would such sensational criminal behavior not be tolerated, but the perpetrators of such violence would be punished in such a way that went far beyond simple incarceration.

What becomes most immediately apparent in the example of Alcatraz as a state of exception is the way in which this new facility suspends the normative use of solitary confinement. Fundamentally fueled by the realization that these super criminals no longer fit within the existing political system, a specific facility was required to not only separate these individuals from civil society, but to separate them from the society of captives as well. Such a strategy became particularly necessary given the way in which certain segments of society socially constructed their actions relative to the legitimacy of the existing social order.

What made the structure of Alcatraz so different from the existing federal system of penitentiaries was the way in which it incorporated restricted confinement as a general practice throughout the institution. A prisoner entering this facility was introduced to a daily routine that was likely not all that different from those individuals entering the penitentiary at Auburn, New York, nearly 100 years earlier. "While the prisoners protested the conditions of confinement from the beginning, daily life at Alcatraz changed very little over the three decades it was in operation" (Ward & Werlich, 2003, p. 55). As was discussed above,

Alcatraz reflects what Agamben (2015/2014) described as the double action of the instrument.

Viewed from this perspective, Alcatraz reflects the causal instrumentality of a type of use or action that derives from the rationale of the principal actor of criminal justice along with the proper action such a structure evokes. Devised as a symbolic response to the growing threat posed by these "super criminals," Alcatraz exemplified the dual function of this type of instrumentality. As a proper form, it sufficiently addressed the needed architectural function for this extreme manifestation of correctional incarceration, while at the same time powerfully articulating the desired intent of this example of rationalized retribution.

However, by the late 1950s new perspectives concerning the relationship between incarceration and rehabilitation began to emerge, challenging the utility of the continued use of Alcatraz. The penal strategy at Alcatraz and the extreme conditions that this type of environment created were viewed as anachronistic, and counterproductive in their results. From this new evolving perspective, Alcatraz served no purpose, particularly if all it could deliver was punishment, which would almost certainly make the inmate worse. Within the emerging correctional environment of psychological programming intended to address and correct a variety of psychological "flaws" now believed related to criminal behavior, Alcatraz no longer served any useful purpose in the realization of this newly recognized goal and was ultimately closed in 1963 (Ward & Werlich, 2003). Within a few short months, the federal prison at Marion, IL was opened.

If Alcatraz was envisioned to address the difficulties evoked by the presence of the super criminal, the Marion penitentiary was to usher in the age of offender rehabilitation. Central to this "rehabilitative" ideology was the application of the behavioral modification approach of Skinnerian operant conditioning (Richards, 2015). As a clinical model of psychotherapeutic intervention, operant conditioning was based on the premise that behavioral change occurred when problematic behavior was replaced by an environmentally desired alternative. To achieve this result, the inmate client would be given cigarettes or some other valued reward when they performed the desired behavior. Over time, this behavior would be modified, due to the regular employment of positive reinforcement, until the unwanted behavior had been extinguished. Central to this theoretical perspective was the belief that human behavior was a predicate of environmental conditioning and, as a result, susceptible to change.

Given that operant conditioning theorized that the individual was exclusively shaped by environmental cues, it was hypothesized that this approach could be particularly beneficial for incarcerated inmates. Such a theoretical approach seemed well suited to the penitentiary given that most inmates were believed to come from a variety of criminogenic environments. As a result, the controlled conditions of incarcerated existence seemed well suited to this type of behavioral change. However, as Richards (2015) has powerfully observed, the Marion experiment did little more than transform prisoners into lab rats, using the techniques of operant conditioning to manipulate compliance (Richards, 2015).

It is not surprising that the "Marion experiment" within approximately the span of a decade lost all credibility as a model of rehabilitation and became identified more with the worst types of unethical "treatment" practices evidenced by the forced medication of prisoners, brainwashing, and various inhumane forms of social isolation (Richards, 2015). By the early 1980s it became known as one of the most notorious penitentiaries in the US correctional system and could be legitimately identified as an example of a state of exception. Though Marion was initially introduced to represent a new era in offender rehabilitation, it became in rather short order a more technologically advanced version of the utility of rationalized retribution it was created to replace.

It is important to recognize that though the Marion experiment was intended to replace the harsh environment of Alcatraz, all it ultimately accomplished was to introduce a different example of rationalized retribution. However, unlike the previous iterations of this dynamic, Marion's initial "rehabilitative promise" was motivated by the emerging influence of psychiatric pharmacological interventions and the therapeutic prominence of Skinner's operant conditioning (Minor & Baumgardner, 2015; Richards, 2015). It was believed that this new approach to offender rehabilitation would correct the failures of the past, as represented by the extreme conditions of Alcatraz, while ushering in a new set of strategies that could be successfully employed in transforming the most difficult of inmates into productive citizens. Unfortunately this reasoning has been shown to be tragically wrong.

The failure of the Marion experiment, much like those correctional rehabilitative failures of the past, all seem to exemplify a similar difficulty or flaw: the inability to incorporate a strategy of rehabilitation within a context of punishment. As a result, and regardless of the actual intent of this rational process, the retributive characteristics of these approaches were clearly reflected in the strategies employed. Furthermore, as these hypothesized rehabilitative goals became compromised by the underlying manifestation of these utilities of retribution, a more punitive institutional response was imposed. However, rather than exploring the ways in which the structure of this process contributed to these failures, the institutional disorder and the brutal violence that followed were used as evidence with which to justify more extreme strategies of control.

It will be recalled that this chapter began with a brief discussion of MacIntyre's (1988) observation, which stated that "… domination of a certain kind is in fact the cause of those characteristics of the dominated which are then evoked to justify unjustified domination" (p. 105). Whether we apply this observation to the deleterious effects of solitary confinement described by Cleveland over 150 years ago (Toch, 2003) or the negative effects of this process documented in Danish prisons from 1870 to 1920 (Smith, 2008), or the more recent documentation of penitentiaries like Marion (Crewe, 2011; Levin, 2014; Richards, 2015), it seems reasonable to conclude that domination of this type has been responsible for the fabrication of those characteristics in those dominated to "justify unjustified domination."

Once these characteristics become manifest as a problem or crisis, the necessity which they evoke ushers in yet another example of a state of exception. However, this "necessity" may be recognized as an ongoing process or ever-present threat that allows this exception to be situated within the law itself. Once this occurs, an ongoing state of exception exists, thereby contextualizing this necessity as an ongoing political-legal fact that is embraced and rationalized by the law.

As a recurrent constructed necessity, the use of solitary confinement continues to flourish as a core strategy of correctional control. Whenever the benefit of this brand of correctional practice has been challenged by the facts of its own failure, this utility of necessity has been called upon time and again to justify its continued existence. Even in the aftermath of the spectacular failure of the Marion experiment, the use of isolated confinement has expanded and has become a more or less common practice across the federal and state correctional systems in the United States and elsewhere. However, it is important to recognize that this expansion is not confined to the traditional practice of solitary confinement; rather, it reflects the troubling fact that this type of incarceration strategy is being used as a general institutional policy imposed on an entire penitentiary population. Though the more traditional forms of disciplinary control are still employed, the new supermax facilities are configured by varying degrees of extreme isolation that have ushered in the newest iteration of the correctional utility of rationalized retribution. An example of this dynamic is witnessed in what Haney (2008) has described as the "ecology of cruelty."

The supermax penitentiary, rationalized retribution, and the ecology of cruelty

Though much has been written concerning the various ways in which the instrumental causality of supermax incarceration imposes a phenomenology of harm on those placed in this type of incarcerated setting, much less has been offered concerning the influence this phenomenological context has on correctional staff working within those institutions. In his article, "A Culture of Harm: Taming the Dynamics of Cruelty in Supermax Prisons," Haney (2008) explores the various ways in which the structural harm of this type of confinement evokes an ecology of cruelty from those individuals who work in these institutional environments. Haney (2008) observes that the structural mistreatment of prisoners identified by this type of confinement, also helps to "… create a heightened probability of mistreatment, ranging from deliberate indifference to outright brutality" (p. 958). As a zone of indifference, supermax confinement is rationally intended to deny the basic necessities of human existence, literally attempting to "unhinge" the most basic foundations of human experience (Guenther, 2013). It could be argued, in fact, that such a penal philosophy serves no other real purpose (Crewe, 2011; Kupers, 2014, 2016). It is therefore not all that surprising that penitentiary staff who are exposed to these normative strategies of mistreatment act toward the prisoners under their custody and control in ways which reflect the structural intentionality of these total confinement institutions.

When Haney (2008) observes that "The potential for significant abuse inheres in the very structure of a prison (p. 958)," he is identifying the way in which the prison context facilitates the socially constructed attitudes and practices of those within that "normative" milieu. If those who find themselves incarcerated in this type of correctional setting are constructed as the worst of the worse, as morally irremediable, or ontologically predatory or threatening, those normative practices, which emerge as a result of this meaning-generating process, will likely reflect the brutality and mistreatment that Haney contends become inevitable within the day-to-day interactions between prison staff and the inmate population. Once such a philosophical position has been constructed, and these taken-for-granted formulations of this "criminal other" become normativity validated, what follows will often be viewed as beyond moral reproach (Agamben, 1995/1998; Polizzi, 2016). In fact, it helps to evoke what Arendt (2006) has defined as the banality of evil.

The banality of evil, driven by neither ideological certainty nor deliberate malice, emerges as an obligation to one's duty to the "normative" functioning of a given organization or institution. For the criminal justice professional working in this type of correctional setting, the structural cruelties of this type of confinement seem to invite a mirroring of that cruelty, which is often articulated within the regular interaction with inmates. Indifference or brutality toward inmates is not only rarely sanctioned, but is accepted as the normative standard by which these relationships should be viewed. In fact, those individuals who refuse to accept this "normative standard" are often viewed with suspicion.

From this perspective, the state of exception not only creates zones of indifference, which blur the lines of demarcation between the law and the political order, but similarly constructs localities of harm, whereby a specific type of ontological construction and epistemological practice become "normatively" consistent with these environmental contexts. If, for example, the convicted criminal is now viewed as being somehow less than human, as reflecting a category of human being that is configured as being ontologically Other (Levinas, 1961/1969), it seems to logically follow that the architectural design of these facilities and the strategies employed to contain and control such individuals will also reflect this ontological conclusion (Haney, 2009). The call for the end of such facilities and their isolating correctional practices, based on Eighth Amendment concerns related to cruel and unusual punishment, have for the most part failed, not because of the ethical imperative involved in such appeals, but due to the fact that the law no longer applies to these incarcerated individuals in the same way (or until a different perspective from the court can emerge).

As an example of bare life, as described by Agamben (1995/1998) these individuals find themselves as the targets of state-sponsored violence, manifested by the expanding use of supermax incarceration. Often economically and politically marginalized prior to incarceration, these citizen-refugees reflect a category of life that finds itself "stateless" within its own society.

Though it is constantly assumed that the Constitution does not stop at the penitentiary door, the state of exception evoked by this type of incarceration blurs the demarcation of its actual application and reach. The state of exception reflected in such "legal" examples as indeterminate detention without charge for suspected terrorists at the prison at Guantanamo Bay, American citizens being executed by

Presidential decree for involvement in terrorist activities, the use of "enhanced interrogation" or torture or state authorized rendition, all exist within the same blurring of the juridical order that selectively recognizes each as a zone of indifference legitimated by the utility of rationalized retribution (Agamben, 2005/2003). The supermax penitentiary becomes a similar artifact of this type of meaning-generating process.

However, what becomes most recognizable between the process of "normal" incarceration and the instrumental causality evoked by supermax confinement is that in this latter example of correctional control, the strategy of rehabilitation has been abandoned. Once constructed as irredeemable or ontologically incapable of rehabilitative change, the utility of rationalized retribution is evoked with little concern for the institutional harm such strategies impose. Whereas the rehabilitative machine seeks to re-fabricate the "criminal" self, into a more docile and controllable self, the strategy of the supermax machine is to annihilate self, and contain what remains of this process within the alien confines of isolated custody (Lanier, Polizzi, & Wade, 2014; Polizzi, Draper, & Andersen, 2014).

It is important to note that not all involvement in these highly restrictive correctional environments results in the extreme consequences implied above; but neither should this fact be used to diminish the profound effect such types of incarceration has on those who experience this type of correctional control. As Haney (2008) observed:

> [T]here are better and worse supermaxes including some that seek to ameliorate these harsh conditions and minimize the harm to prisoners. And there are more and less resilient prisoners, including some who seem able to withstand the painfulness of these environments and to recover from the experience with few lasting effects. But neither fact challenges the overall consensus that has emerged on the harmfulness of long-term punitive isolation and the risks to prisoners who are subjected to it (p. 956).

Though it is difficult to disagree with the contention that an overall consensus exists concerning the punitive effects of long-term isolation, that fact, however, has been less successful in actually ending this type of correctional practice. Mentally ill inmates have found some relief through the courts, which have begun to exclude the use of supermax confinement for the most psychologically vulnerable inmates. However, regardless these successes, solitary confinement and its more contemporary manifestation, the supermax prison, remain central features of a penal philosophy defined by the utility of rationalized retribution. In the face of such incriminating evidence concerning the documented ill-effects of this type of confinement, one would think that a constitutional challenge based on Eighth Amendment protections against cruel and unusual punishment would be able to successfully bring these practices to an end in the United States. Unfortunately that result has not been achieved. We will now move to a brief discussion of the role of the US Supreme Court as it relates to solitary confinement, supermax penitentiaries, and cruel and unusual punishment.

THE SUPREME COURT, SOLITARY CONFINEMENT, AND THE PROHIBITION OF CRUEL AND UNUSUAL PUNISHMENT

The Eighth Amendment and its applicability to the states

The history of the relationship between the use of solitary confinement and its potential violation of the constitutional protection against cruel and unusual punishment, as established by the Eighth Amendment of the US Constitution goes back to 1866. One of the initial obstacles in establishing this relationship centered on the jurisdictional applicability of the Bill of Rights as this related to established state law. It was initially argued that the Bill of Rights with its various constitutional protections was the exclusive legal domain of all federal jurisdictions, but did not hold a similar claim on the states. From 1866 to 1892 a number of cases were argued before the Supreme Court with the intent of establishing the degree to which federal constitutional protections could be applied to the states.

In all of the cases argued before the court during this 26-year period, only the decision offered in *In re Medley*, 1890 established some small degree of protection against cruel and unusual punishment claims.

In that case, Medley had been convicted of murder in Colorado and was sentenced to death for his crime. Subsequent to his conviction, a state statute was enacted that required all condemned inmates to be housed in solitary confinement until execution. The court argued that such a stipulation imposed an additional punishment after conviction and therefore amounted to a double penalty that exceeded the legal authority of the state (Rovner, 2016). Given that the requirement of solitary confinement inflicted a greater degree of punishment than was imposed at sentencing, Medley's claim that the statute violated his Eighth Amendment right was affirmed and the additional punishment of solitary confinement was vacated by the court (*In re Medley*, 1890).

However, in four other cases argued before the court during the same period of years, attempts to extend Eighth Amendment protections to state jurisdictions were denied. In *Pervear v. The Commonwealth*, 1866, *In re Kemmler*, 1890, *McElvaine v. Brush*, 1891, and *O'Neil v. Vermont*, 1898, the court on each occasion ruled that protection from cruel and unusual punishment as guaranteed by the Eighth Amendment of the US Constitution did not extend to state jurisdictions. In *Pervear*, the court rejected the claim that certain sentencing practices employed by The Common Wealth of Massachusetts constituted the claim of cruel and unusual punishment. In *In re Kemmler*, the court held that execution by electrocution – newly introduced as a more humane method of execution – did not violate the Eighth Amendment and in fact agreed that this new method of execution was more humane and therefore could not be considered cruel per the wording in the Constitution.

> It implies there something inhuman and barbarous, – something more than the mere extinguishment of life. The courts of New York held that the mode adopted in this instance might be said to be unusual because it is new, but that it could not be assumed to be cruel in the light of that common knowledge which has stamped certain punishments as such. (*In re Kemmler*, 1890).

What is perhaps most interesting or troubling in the logic offered in *In re Kemmler* is that the court does not seem to argue that the Eighth Amendment is not applicable to the states, only that the state's decision to introduce a new method of execution – death by electrocution – does not rise to the level of cruel and unusual punishment. In fact, it could perhaps be argued that the decision in *In re Kemmler* establishes the theoretical applicability of the Eighth Amendment to the states, while at the very same time undermining the practical application of that decision. Given that execution likely represented the most extreme example of "ethically challenged" correctional practice, little was actually gained in this theoretical victory.

The court reaffirmed its ruling in *In re Kemmler* a year later and rejected the claim made in *McElvaine* that New York's use of electrocution and solitary confinement rose to the level of cruel and unusual punishment. Employing much of the same logic offered in *In re Kemmler*, the court concluded that the method of execution and the use of solitary confinement resided solely with the judgment of the New York legislature. In so doing, the court also returned to the logic it offered in *In re Medley* concerning the imposition of solitary confinement and the death penalty. Though the facts of these two cases seemed similar, the court disagreed.

In *McElvaine*, the plaintiff claimed that it was contesting a similar issue that was favorably resolved in *Medley*; however, this was in fact not true. Whereas in *Medley* the inclusion of the stipulation for solitary confinement was the result of a statute which was passed after conviction and therefore was viewed by the court as an unauthorized additional punishment, this circumstance was not present in *McElvaine*. In *McElvaine*, statutory authority had been included in the New York Criminal Code and therefore there was no legitimate claim that solitary confinement could be construed as an after-conviction punishment such as that prohibited in *Medley*.

It was not until *Weems v. U.S.* that the Court took up the proportionality principle of the Eighth Amendment. The proportionality principle is generally concerned with the degree to which the severity of the crime is compatible with the severity of the punishment imposed by the law. Included in this determination is the degree to which evolving social standards should be considered when arriving at such a conclusion (Ginwalla, 1992). Though the Court clearly recognized the right of the legislature to define crimes and their punishment, it argued that it is the duty of the judiciary to determine whether the legislature has "… contravened a constitutional prohibition …" (*Weems v. U.S.*, 1910).

> In Eighth Amendment jurisprudence, the opinions reflect moral and philosophical differences as to the purposes of punishment (whether a retributivist or utilitarian model is more appropriate). The Justices also disagree as to whether a changing moral consensus in society should yield different standards for evaluating cruel and unusual punishment. The decision reflects the Court's continuing struggle to interpret the cruel and unusual punishment clause in the Eighth Amendment (Ginwalla, 1992, p. 607).

As the above discussion reveals, the strategy to extend Eighth Amendment protections to the states has been forced to confront a variety of legal challenges, many of which have ultimately been defeated in the Supreme Court. Over the last 25 years a similar number of legal challenges have been waged concerning the appropriate application of the cruel and unusual punishment provision of the Eighth Amendment with similarly mixed results. As Ginwalla (1992) has observed, the application of the cruel and unusual punishment provision has needed to struggle with the philosophical purposes of punishment and the changing moral consensus in society as this relates to how the legal construct of cruel and unusual punishment should actually be defined.

Central to this debate has been whether or not the changing moral consensus of society should be employed as the measuring stick by which cruel and unusual punishments should be determined. On one side of this debate are those who embrace the original intent perspective famously employed by the late Antonin Scalia, which holds that the Constitution should only be interpreted per the original intent of the Framers. On the other side of this debate are those who view the Constitution as a living document and as such, one that must reflect the current moral consensus of contemporary society. Perhaps nowhere has this struggle found more significance than in the jurisprudence related to the death penalty. Though a thorough exploration of the question concerning the relationship between the application of the cruel and unusual punishment provision and the death penalty is well beyond the scope of the current discussion, its inclusion will help to better situate the questions concerning cruel and unusual punishment and solitary and supermax confinement.

Cruel and unusual punishment and the death penalty

In 1972 the Supreme Court ruled in their landmark decision in *Furman v. Georgia* that the arbitrary nature of the sentencing process in capital cases resulted in a violation of the cruel and unusual punishment provision of the Eighth Amendment of the US Constitution (*Furman v. Georgia*, 1972). As a result of this decision, 40 state death penalty statutes were immediately voided, all current occupants of death row nationwide had their sentences commuted and the use of the death penalty was suspended given that statutes allowing its use were no longer legally valid (Death Penalty Information Center, 2016; *Furman v. Georgia*, 1972). It is important to note that though nine different justices offered opinions in this case, the vote was 5–4 favoring the suspension of death penalty statutes nationwide; only Justices Brennan and Marshall actually opined that the death penalty was unconstitutional (Death Penalty Information Center, 2016).

In the aftermath of *Furman*, 34 states sought to have the availability of the death penalty reinstated. Given that the main focus of the court's decision targeted the arbitrary nature of death penalty statutes, death penalty proponents immediately went to work to address this concern. Their initial attempt removed all of the discretionary language from a number of state death penalty statutes and replaced this with a required mandatory capital sentence for all those individuals convicted of a capital crime (Death Penalty Information Center, 2016). However, when these statutory revisions were placed before the court, they were also found to be unconstitutional (*Woodson v. North Carolina*, 1976).

In overturning the North Carolina death penalty statute, the court observed that the law provided no guidelines for the jury concerning who would be eligible to receive the death penalty and who would not. The court continued by stating that the automatic application of such a result without the consideration of those circumstances specific to convicted individuals evoked the cruel and unusual punishment provision of the Eighth Amendment, therefore rendering the statute unconstitutional (*Woodson v. North Carolina*, 1976). However, much like the court's decision in *Furman*, the constitutionality of the death penalty was not questioned and as a result left open the possibility for its reinstatement. A few months after the court rendered their opinion in *Woodson*, another case was before the court attempting to reinstate the death penalty.

In *Gregg v. Georgia*, the court once again took up the issue of reinstating the death penalty; however, unlike previous attempts, this case was successful and the death penalty was reinstated. In this ruling, the majority once again upheld the constitutionality of the death penalty by asserting that it did not in all circumstances violate the cruel and unusual punishment provision of the Eighth Amendment (*Gregg v. Georgia*, 1976). Having satisfied the difficulties raised in *Furman* concerning the arbitrary application of a capital sentence, the statute was ruled to be constitutional (*Gregg v. Georgia*, 1976). However, though reinstated, this did not end the debate concerning the death penalty and its potential violation of Eighth Amendment protections against cruel and unusual punishment.

In the aftermath of *Gregg v. Georgia*, the debate concerning the death penalty and the Eighth Amendment took a slightly different turn. If *Furman*, *Woodson*, and *Gregg* challenged the constitutionality of the statutory language used to apply a capital sentence, a number of death penalty cases from the late 1980s through 2006 sought to determine the sentencing eligibility of certain groups based on age or level of psychological functioning. In each of these cases the cruel and unusual punishment provision was evoked relative to its applicability and its relationship to evolving standards of decency. The first of these cases addressed the issue of age as it related to the defendant's eligibility to receive a capital sentence.

In *Stanford v. Kentucky*, 1989, the court took up the constitutionality of sentencing to death a defendant who was 17 years old at the time of the homicide. Stanford claimed that the sentence of death violated the cruel and unusual punishment provision of the Eighth Amendment, given that his case should not have been waived to adult court and he should be allowed the opportunity of rehabilitation based on his age at the time of crime. In a 5–4 vote, the court disagreed and ruled to uphold the conviction. In his majority opinion, Justice Scalia famously argued that for a punishment to be considered cruel and unusual and therefore unconstitutional, it would have to be so considered when the Bill of Rights was adopted or would have to conflict with evolving standards of decency (*Stafford v. Kentucky*, 1989).

In *Atkins v. Virginia*, 2002, the court explored the issue concerning whether or not an intellectually disabled – formerly mentally retarded – defendant could be considered eligible for the death penalty. In writing for the majority, Justice Stevens ruled that the sentencing of a defendant with severe intellectual disability – formally mental retardation – violated the protection against excessive punishment and seemed to violate evolving moral stands concerning the sentencing of such an individual. To support his argument, Stevens pointed to the fact that a growing consensus now exists among the states as well as the federal government that a capital sentence should be specifically prohibited for those defendants diagnosed with a severe intellectual disability.

In 2005, the Court revisited its decision concerning the eligibility of the death penalty for a defendant who was 17 years old at the time of the crime. In *Roper v. Simmons*, the Court ruled that sentencing a 17-year-old defendant to death violated the cruel and unusual punishment provision of the Eighth Amendment and therefore overruled the defendant's capital conviction. Central to this argument was the fact that adolescent decision-making was less developed than it was in adults, and therefore required a different degree of proportionality as this related to capital sentence eligibility (*Roper v. Simmons*, 2005). The majority also observed that evolving standards of decency relating to juvenile eligibility for the death penalty had changed significantly since the court's decision in *Stanford*. As a result, the court upheld the decision of the Missouri Supreme Court and vacated the defendant's capital sentence; by so doing, the court overturned the ruling provided in *Stanford* and established that a defendant now must be 18 years old at the time of the crime to be eligible for a capital sentence (*Roper v. Simmons*, 2005).

What these cases reveal is the evolving definitional context in which the phrase "cruel and unusual punishment" will be constructed. The answer to this question no longer seems to revolve around whether or not the Eighth Amendment is applicable to the states; rather, the current focus of the court – as established in the cases discussed above – appears more concerned with how this definition will be applied. As was powerfully exemplified in *Atkins* and *Roper*, the court's decisions in these cases reflect a desire to focus on certain groups deemed to be potentially most vulnerable to protections guaranteed by the Eighth Amendment. The issue of vulnerability is a particularly pertinent one when applied to the practice of solitary and supermax confinement.

Solitary and supermax confinement and the Eighth Amendment

Whereas the court has ruled in recent decisions that certain populations, due to characteristics specific to them, are ineligible to receive a capital sentence, that sentence that same codification of vulnerability has not been applied with the same clarity when applied to the practice of solitary and supermax confinement. When these cases have reached the US Supreme Court, generally under the auspices of an alleged violation of Eighth and Fourteenth Amendment protections prohibiting the use of cruel and unusual punishment or infractions related to due process rights, the position offered from the bench has consistently reflected an unwillingness to get into the business of prison administration, which the jurists have constantly argued falls under the legitimate purview of penitentiary authorities (*Martin v. Hadix*, 1999; *Sandin v. Conner*, 1995; *Wilkinson v. Austin*, 2005). Though the court has consistently maintained that the Eighth Amendment is constitutionally applicable to a variety of penitentiary conditions, including the use of solitary confinement, it has failed to rule that such a practice is unconstitutional in all instances (Wedekind, 2011). However, in certain cases it has ruled on what will not be allowed.

In *Brooks v. Florida*, 1967, the court heard a case concerning the conviction of three individuals who had been charged and sentenced for participating in a prison riot. Once prison authorities regained control of the institution, all three plaintiffs were ordered to serve 35 days in a punishment cell. The cell was 7 feet long and 6½ feet wide, with no window to the outside and no bed or other furnishings, and the occupants were forced to use a hole in the cell floor for the bathroom (*Brooks v. Florida*, 1967). After enduring 15 days of these harsh conditions, which included a ration of 4 ounces of soup three times a day and an 8-ounce ration of water, Brooks confessed to his involvement in the riot. The trial judge, who was well aware of the conditions of confinement, still concluded the confession was voluntary. The court disagreed.

In a 9–0 decision, the court overruled the lower court on the grounds that the confession was a product of torture and voided the conviction. So clear was the court's decision that it failed even to address the other concerns raised by the plaintiff. "The record in this case documents a shocking display of barbarism which should not escape the remedial action of this Court. Accordingly, we reverse the judgement below" (*Brooks v. Florida*, 1967). Though the court's ruling in *Brooks* had no difficulty in recognizing the barbaric conditions employed to evoke a confession, the result of that decision has had little impact in more recent cases concerning the constitutionality of solitary and supermax confinement.

In *Sandin v. Conner*, 1995, the court took up the issue concerning whether or not the plaintiff was denied due process when he was refused the possibility of presenting witnesses at his disciplinary custody hearing, a constitutional due process protection established in *Wolff v. McDonnell*, 1974. The court rejected this argument by ruling that Connor incorrectly claimed that "... any state action taken for a punitive reason ..." violated the Due Process Clause and that placement in segregated custody, did not "... inevitability affect the duration of his sentence, since the chance that the misconduct finding will affect his parole status is simply too attenuated to invoke the Due Process Clause's procedural guarantees" (*Sandin v. Conner*, 1995).

In *Wilkinson v. Austin* (2005) the issue before the court was focused on whether or not the Ohio placement system for inclusion into their supermax facility violated the due process rights of those inmates assigned to that penitentiary. Though the court carefully outlined the conditions of this type of incarceration, noting many of the implications of the same, and also recognized that the placement process was at times haphazardly applied, they still concluded "... that the procedures Ohio has adopted provide sufficient procedural protection to comply with due process requirement" (*Wilkinson v. Austin*, 2005).

Perhaps the most relevant court finding in this discussion as it relates to solitary confinement and the cruel and unusual punishment provision of the Eighth Amendment is the decision offered in *Wilson v. Seiter*, 1991. In that case, the plaintiff argued that the conditions of his confinement constituted cruel and unusual punishment, therefore requiring remediation by prison authorities, who failed to do so (*Wilson v. Seiter*, 1991). However, in rejecting that claim, the court ruled that Wilson failed to establish the culpability of prison officials. "A prisoner claiming that the conditions of his confinement violate the Eighth Amendment must show a culpable state of mind on the part of prison officials" (*Wilson v. Seiter*, 1991). As a result, the court established a two-prong standard by which penitentiary claims of cruel and unusual punishment would be determined.

The standard established by the court included both an objective and subjective component. The objective component of this standard requires that prison conditions be perilous enough to "... pose a substantial risk of serious harm" (Goldman & Brimmer, 2016). The subjective component of this standard requires that prison officials were deliberately indifferent to the risk created by such conditions and disregarded the potential harm inflicted on prisoners in a given institution (*Wilson v. Seiter*, 1991). Though the court ruled against the claims made by Wilson, it does appear that the "logic" of the court is somewhat strained concerning its rationale.

If we return to the discussion of instrumental causality provided in Chapter three, it becomes possible to examine the philosophical implications that the court's logic seems to evoke. It will be recalled that Agamben (2015/2014) defined instrumental causality as that which acts by virtue of a principal agent and by virtue of the specific nature of the instrument. If we were to apply the construct of instrumental causality to the logic offered by the court in *Wilson*, the objective component of solitary confinement would be recognized by the serious harm that it may inflict, which in turn reflects the proper form of the instrument by virtue of the harm it imposes when in use. The subjective component of solitary confinement would be reflected by the principal agent of the criminal justice system, which continues to impose the conditions of this practice on prisoners from an attitude of indifference – rationalized retribution – which for the most part continually ignores the well-documented harms this type of correctional practice evokes (Arrigo, Bersot & Sellers, 2011; Guenther, 2013; Haney, 2008; Haney, Weill, Bakhshay, & Lockett, 2015; Pizarro & Stenius, 2004; Richards, 2008; Shalev, 2011). Viewed from this perspective, the instrumental causality of solitary confinement appears to satisfy both components required by the court to determine a plaintiff's claim of cruel and unusual punishment: the imposition of serious harm and the attitudinal indifference of the same by prison authorities.

When attempting to apply the construct of instrumental causality to the apparatus of solitary confinement, it is important to recognize that the function of the instrument – in this case the specific structural aspects of the solitary confinement cell – can only inflict harm when the principal agent uses the instrument as intended by it: that is, as an intentional instrument of harm which only becomes manifest through the intentional action of the principal agent. Though the structural configuration of the solitary confinement cell seems to evoke a daunting array of punishing qualities, this possibility can only be realized when used in a way that is not specific to its nature: that is, when employed by the criminal justice system to evoke a specific utility of rationalized retribution.

For example, the solitary confinement cell, regardless its diminished space, remains just that and does not become an instrument of harm until it is used as an instrument of rationalized retribution. Only when the proper form of the instrument is situated within the intentional horizon of the principal actor does it become transformed into an instrument of intentional harm. Left to its own design, and returning to its proper form, the possibility for cruelty to be evoked by the solitary confinement cell is neutralized: a dormant horizontal possibility that exists beyond the nature of this tiny configured space.

If the possibility of the serious harm attributed to solitary confinement is not specifically present in its proper form as a space of confinement, what then does this reveal concerning the intent of the principal agent of the criminal justice system? In *Wilson* the court argued that "A prisoner claiming that the conditions of his confinement violate the Eighth Amendment must show a culpable state of mind on the part of prison officials" (*Wilson v. Seiter*, 1991). Given that the use of the instrument of solitary confinement can only evoke cruelty if used for the purposes of the same, it seems logical to contend that this practice introduces a continuum of potentially serious harm that is not otherwise institutionally established by other means. It seems difficult to argue, then, that the instrumental causality of this practice is not sufficient to establish "the culpable state of mind" of penitentiary officials as is required by *Wilson*. How could it not?

Though the court has rarely affirmed that solitary confinement rises to the level of cruel and unusual punishment, lower federal and state appellate courts have provided some direction on this issue. In *Madrid v. Gomez*, 1999, The United States Court of Appeals, 9th Circuit took up the question of cruel and unusual punishment as this applied to the Special Housing Unit (SHU) at Pelican Bay penitentiary in California. Whereas inmates claimed that the extreme isolation of the SHU resulted in varying degrees of psychological trauma, the

California Department of Correction – as it was then called – argued that the plaintiffs were unable to show any instrumental causality between unit conditions and mental illness (Shalev, 2011). Not completely arguing with either of these claims, the court observed:

> We are not persuaded that the SHU, as currently operated violates Eighth Amendment standards vis-à-vis all inmates. We do find, however, that conditions in the SHU violate such standards when imposed on certain subgroups of the inmate population, and that defendants have been deliberately indifferent to the serious risks posed by subjecting such inmates to the SHU over extended periods of time (*Madrid v. Gomez*, 1999, p. 1261).

In *Madrid*, the court ultimately refused to find the practice of solitary confinement completely lacking in "… *any* penological justification (Shalev, 2011, p. 163). It reasoned that though brief periods of confinement may induce a degree of psychological trauma that experience would not be sufficient to rise to the level of cruel and unusual punishment (Shalev, 2011). However, the court did recognize that for mentally ill individuals or those vulnerable to same, such conditions posed a serious threat of harm and revealed an attitude of indifference on the part of prison authorities that, when used with such prisoners, earned the designation of cruel and unusual punishment. The court powerfully observed that "If the particular conditions of segregation being challenged are such that they inflict a serious mental illness, greatly exacerbate mental illness, or deprive inmates of a basic necessity of human existence … indeed, they have crossed in to the realm of psychological torture" (*Madrid v. Gomez*, 1999, p. 1264).

Though the significance of this ruling should not be underemphasized as it relates to those inmates who are now constitutionally protected against such practices, it does leave open the debate concerning those inmates not covered by this ruling. Given that the court ruled that brief periods of disciplinary custody and the accompanying psychological trauma evoked do not rise to the level of cruel and unusual punishment, how is the demarcation between brief and long-term confinement established? Furthermore, if this "continuum of cruelty" is one of the mechanisms by which constitutionally prohibited cruelty is recognized, how is that factor established? But even if we could agree that the intentionality of the principal agent clearly reveals a culpable state of mind as this relates to the actual use of solitary confinement, we would still be required to answer another question: But is this practice unusual?

The unusualness standard of the cruel and unusual punishment provision of the Eighth Amendment provides a far more difficult challenge to overcome. As Justice Scalia has argued, a specific correctional practice may indeed be cruel, but because it is not unusual, it is therefore not an example of a violation of Eighth Amendment protections. From this perspective, it is difficult to imagine how solitary confinement could ever be viewed as "unusual," given that it has been a core aspect of US correctional practice since the very inception of the penitentiary. However, perhaps if we explore the construct of "unusual" from a different perspective that challenge becomes less daunting.

Traditionally, for a correctional practice to be deemed unusual, it must exist so far outside the normative imagination of legal sensibility that it comes to reflect a type of conceptual brutality that so overwhelms conventional thought that it must not be allowed to continue: within the context of the current discussion, *Brooks v. Florida*, 1967 seems to fit that example. However, in its most general sense, that same type of logic has really never applied to the use of solitary confinement, except in a few specific instances. Though the use of this practice was viewed as inappropriate as a legitimate mechanism of rehabilitative change, that realization was not sufficient to end the practice. And in fact, this is where the construction of solitary confinement, as both a cruel and "usual" form of punishment comes to emerge as a state of exception.

One of the most problematic consequences of the incorporation of a state of exception is that over time it gains both legal and political legitimacy (Agamben, 2005/2003). Once so instituted, the zone of indifference that this process creates becomes a functioning part of the larger legal-political landscape. Though the military prison at

Guantanamo Bay, Cuba, was viewed as a clear violation of many of the bedrock principles of American legal due process (Agamben, 2005/2003; Arrigo & Bersot, 2014; Ek, 2006; Murray, 2010) it continues to receive political support today from those who have fought to keep this facility open. As an intentionally crafted zone of indifference, Guantanamo Bay comes to encompass what would be legally unacceptable and politically untenable in American society, while remaining "useful" and "usual" as an apparatus in the War on Terror. However, how is it that we arrive at the conclusion that a certain construct reflects what is usual?

Generally speaking, what we consider to be usual is that which is cognitively present as something that is common and recognizable. We are aware, for example, that the practice of solitary confinement has been with us for well over 200 years; however, does that fact render it usual? The answer to that question appears to be yes. It is rendered usual by defaulting to the durational presence of this practice. It will be recalled that Justice Scalia has argued that the death penalty, for example, must be viewed as constitutional given that this practice was in use at the time that the Constitution was being written. He not only further argued that this practice is constitutional, but also observed that the use of the death penalty was employed far more broadly then it is today (*Stanford v. Kentucky*, 1989). However, does this logic necessarily establish a definition for "usual" that is ethically applicable to the question of solitary confinement?

Given that the instrumental causality of solitary confinement is configured by an intentionality that seeks to disrupt the very ontological ground of *usual* human experience, it becomes rather easy to conclude that such a practice is indeed ethically and philosophically unusual. It will be recalled that Cleveland's analysis of the effects of solitary confinement on those prisoners held at the Rhode Island penitentiary in 1845 concluded much the same (Toch, 2003). Central to his critique was the way in which this profoundly unusual correctional context disrupted the ontological foundation and relationality of *usual* human perception and experience. Similar conclusions have been reached by contemporary analysis concerning the "continuum of cruelty" exhibited by the practice of solitary confinement (Arrigo, Bersot & Sellers, 2011; Arrigo & Milovanovic, 2009; Guenther, 2013; Haney, 2008; Kupers, 2014; Shalev, 2009, 2011; Toch, 1992, 2003). As a result, it could be argued that the cruelty of solitary confinement has been documented to be relatable to the highly unusual nature of the conditions of that environment, which in turn become responsible for the "continuum of cruelty" that such a practice facilitates.

It has been argued above that the cruelly unusual aspects of solitary confinement are established by the highly unusual nature of the environment from which they emerge. Structural conditions which drastically restrict the body's comportment, the ability to be in a face-to-face relationship with another human being, or the ability to inhabit a world for any meaningful period of time outside the highly diminished setting of disciplinary custody are so unusually extreme that there is simply no reasonable strategy by which to construct such a process as usual (Guenther, 2013). In fact, if it is true that such disciplinary units are employed as a strategy of deterrence by which to control general population prisoners, the unusual nature of such forms of confinement becomes logically confirmed by that potential threat. Though "normal" prison life is certainly not normal when compared to life on the other side of the penitentiary wall, that comparative difference is greatly enhanced when compared to solitary confinement.

As we will see in the next chapter, one of the more difficult aspects of this experience for those so confined is the way in which the individual constructs the meaning of this encounter with this alien world. Given the extremely unusual conditions of this environment, the very foundations of the self are often thrown into question (Guenther, 2013). Without a normal world in which to engage, the normal capacity for the construction of human meaning is also disrupted. Though the conditions of this type of confinement impose difficult challenges to both physical and psychological health, they are not impossible to overcome in all cases

These strategies of survival have been identified as secondary adjustments (Goffman, 1961), as modes of resistance (Bosworth & Carrabine, 2001; Carrabine, 2004; Crewe, 2007), as agentic friction

(Rubin, 2015), or perhaps as an example of the adjacent possible (Kauffman, 2010). In each of these examples, individuals faced with the reality of disciplinary custody construct a variety of survival strategies that allow them to "tolerate" the extreme and unnatural levels of social isolation. Given that these extreme episodes of disciplinary isolation are intended to erode the integrity of the self by fabricating it into something more docile and controllable, this struggle unfolds at the most foundational levels of human experience (Polizzi, Draper, & Andersen, 2014). Successful resistance, though possible for some, likely depends on the period of time one is forced to endure these conditions (Hartman, 2008).

5

FROM THE OTHER SIDE OF THE DOOR: THE LIVED EXPERIENCE OF SOLITARY CONFINEMENT

In Chapters three and four, the structure and legal construction of the practice of solitary confinement was explored for the purpose of establishing the role that it plays within this phenomenology. What will follow will be a phenomenological exploration of the lived experience of solitary confinement from the narrative accounts in *The Guardian* online newspaper of a group of individuals who have decided to share this experience, from Solitary Watch and its segment on solitary confinement titled *Voices from Solitary*, and other print sources. These first-person narratives not only explore the experience of living in solitary confinement, but also describe how this experience evolves over time.

What these interviews reveal is the lived experience of individuals confronted with the state of exception exemplified by the apparatus of solitary confinement as employed by the criminal justice machine as a strategy for the re-fabrication of the self (Polizzi, Draper & Andersen, 2014). Within this context, Agamben's conceptualization of the apparatus clearly is witnessed. For Agamben (2007/2009), human existence is the struggle between living beings and "… apparatuses in which living beings are incessantly captured" (p. 13). As such, Agamben's conceptualization of the apparatus goes beyond

Foucault's initial formulation of this process. "Further expanding the already large class of Foucauldian apparatuses, I shall call an apparatus literally anything that has in some way the capacity to capture, orient, determine, intercept, model, control, or secure the gestures, behaviors, opinions, or discourses of living beings" (Agamben, 2007/2009, p. 14).

Agamben continues by adding a third class to the initial two categories he provides – living beings and apparatus which he identifies as the subject. "I shall call the subject that which results from the relation and, so to speak, from the relentless fight between living beings and apparatuses" (Agamben, 2007/2009, p. 14). The position of the subject, therefore, emerges from the in-between of this struggle between living being and the apparatus. The process which Agamben describes, however, is threatened by what he calls desubjectification, which is the process that unfolds within our relationship to the apparatus. Our ability to avoid desubjectification begins by first recognizing our relationship to the apparatus, which in turn can evoke a different manifestation of the in-between of living beings and apparatuses (Agamben, 2007/2009).

As Agamben observes, the avoidance of desubjectification is fundamentally predicated on how we take up this relationship to the apparatus. However, if this interaction is a fundamental process of human experience, avoidance and recognition may become difficult to achieve. Even in the most mundane of examples, such as the computer, the cell phone, or social media, living beings often lose themselves to this process of desubjectification, which the relationship to these apparatuses evokes (Agamben, 2007/2009). The apparatus of solitary confinement, though far more severe in its scope, seeks to achieve the same result.

Though the experience of solitary confinement evokes a more familiar Foucauldian relationality between living beings and apparatus, Agamben's attempted triangulation of this process can also be helpful in exploring the phenomenology of this experience. As was stated above, the purpose of this type of isolating confinement is to fundamentally disrupt the basic vectors of human experience in the name of compliance and control. Perhaps stated more simply, such an experience evokes a relationality that is devoid of normal types of human interaction along with a fundamental disruption of bodily comportment. Whether this experience is historically located at the onset of the American penal system or at any other point along this teleological trajectory, certain fundamental aspects or characteristics of normal human relating and normal human existence are denied. What the subsequent interviews reveal is the various strategies by which this disruption is confronted and momentarily overcome.

If the proponents of solitary confinement are unapologetically able to recognize the imposed cruelty of such forms of punishment, why is it still employed as a method of correctional practice? Perhaps the answer to this question can be found in the remarks of Justice Scalia, who famously observed: solitary confinement is certainly cruel but not unusual and is therefore not unconstitutional. If this is true, then perhaps a more appropriate view of solitary confinement can be what Giorgio Agamben has described as the state of exception.

Agamben (2005/2003) describes the philosophical contours of the state of exception in the following way.

> … the state of exception is neither external nor internal to the juridical order, and the problem of defining it concerns precisely a threshold, or zone of indifference, where inside and outside do not exclude each other but rather blur with each other. The suspension of the norm does not mean its abolition, and the zone of anomie that it establishes is not (or at least claims not to be) unrelated to the juridical order (p. 23).

Central to Agamben's configuration of the state of exception is that these zones of indifference neither reflect a total rejection of a particular normative characteristic nor are viewed as somehow unrelated to the juridical order that allows its existence (de la Durantaye, 2009). Solitary confinement reflects both of these definitional characteristics: (1) As a zone of indifference these practices establish a space where such dehumanizing isolation is not only permitted, but (2) rationalized and legitimated by the courts in spite of the acknowledged harm these practices may impose (Hartman, 2008). It is important to note that these zones of indifference are specifically designated to contain those individuals who cannot be otherwise incorporated into the existing political system; a strategy which seems to be also reflected in the proliferation of supermax units that are functionally structured to incapacitate rather than to rehabilitate the inmate populations under their control (Crewe, 2014; Kupers, 2014; Mears & Reisig, 2006).

From this perspective, the state of exception not only creates zones of indifference, by blurring the lines of demarcation between the law and the political order, but also creates a space or locality whereby a specific type of ontological construction and epistemological practice may be employed that is consistent with these environmental contexts. If, for example, the convicted criminal is now viewed as being somehow less than human, whose potential risk identifies them as a category of human being that is configured as ontologically Other (Levinas, 1961/1969), it seems to logically follow that the architecture designed and the strategies employed to contain and control such individuals will also reflect this ontological conclusion (Haney, 2009). The call for the end of such facilities and their isolating correctional practices, based on Amendment concerns related to cruel and unusual punishment must almost certainly fail, not because of the ethical imperative involved in such appeals, but due to the fact that it appears as if the law no longer applies to these incarcerated individuals in the same way.

Once these "exceptions" become reified as rules, more subversive strategies related to the creation of the self remain available and may come to reflect a type of exception to this exception (Lanier, Polizzi, & Wade, 2014). These strategies of survival have been identified as secondary adjustments (Goffman, 1961), as modes of resistance (Bosworth & Carrabine, 2001; Carrabine, 2004; Crewe, 2007), as agentic friction (Rubin, 2015) or as the adjacent possible (Kauffman, 2010). However, as Crewe (2014) and others have pointed out, it would be a mistake to reduce the phenomenology of this type of lived experience to traditional dyadic formulations generally focused on power and resistance.

Embodied subjectivity and the lived space of solitary confinement

In his classic text, *Phenomenology of Perception*, Merleau-Ponty (1945/2012) explores the phenomenology of the lived experience of embodied subjectivity. From this perspective, the body is configured as neither an object in space nor as an extension of a consciousness. Rather, the body is viewed by what Merleau-Ponty has described as a "touching/touchable," which reflects both the ontological materiality of the body; but one that is also endowed by an intentional consciousness. However, the possibility for embodied subjectivity is predicated on its ontological relationality to world. As such, embodied subjectivity finds itself in a world from which the meaning of both becomes possible (Merleau-Ponty, 1945/2012). It is important to recognize that this configuration of body and world is not that of two discrete philosophical categories or an epiphenomenal configuration of the same, which subsumes one as the extension of the other. Rather, much like Heidegger's (2010/1953) construct of being-in-the-world, embodied subjectivity should be viewed as a unified phenomenon that is impossible without a world.

One of the more fundamental aspects of this phenomenology is the way in which embodied subjects experience the contours of the co-constituted dynamic of spatiality. As Barbaras (2006/1999) describes, our ability to experience the spatial relationality of embodied subjectivity and world becomes predicated on the potentiality of living movement. However, from this perspective, the experience of spatial potentiality as this relates to living movement is not that of the encounter between two discrete and objectively separate philosophical constructs. Rather, it configures the point from which spatiality and embodied existence emerge from the ontological ground of this co-constituted experience. The possibility for objective space is rejected – that is, a conceptualization of space that is categorically separate from embodied subjectivity. So if our relationship to space is not that of a container/contained dynamic, how is it configured?

Merleau-Ponty (1945/2012) responds by observing, "Space is not the milieu (real or logical) in which things are laid out, but rather the means by which the position of things become possible" (p. 254). Implicit in this description of space is our embodied relationality to it. Such a relationality is of particular importance to the phenomenology of solitary confinement. If our experience of space is ontologically configured by the position of things, the absence of such possibility can greatly disrupt the ontological grounding for embodied subjectivity.

Anyone having witnessed firsthand the spatial limitations of solitary confinement is immediately struck by just how confining this space actually is. However, the spatial limitations of solitary are not its sole defining characteristic. Included within this context is also a relational and material sparseness that denies virtually all aspects of a normal relationality. Contrast this with the space configured by the phenomenology of hoarding. With hoarding, the individual's lived space becomes overwhelmed by the presence of things. So intrusive is that presence that there is often little room for the individual to take up this space. Just as the experience of hoarding is over-determined by the presence of things, solitary confinement can be defined by an over-determined absence of the same. How then does Merleau-Ponty's analysis of lived space helped to construct the meaning(s) of this experience?

Central to Merleau-Ponty's (1945/2012) analysis of the experience of spatiality is the way in which it situates embodied subjectivity and world. In the experience of solitary confinement, the experience of spatiality is disrupted and "sketches out a spatiality without things" (Merleau-Ponty, 1945/2012, p. 296). In such a profound experience of absence, our anchor to the world is cut from its mooring and its position in that world is no longer secure. "The perception of space is not a particular class of 'states of consciousness' or acts, and its modalities always express the total life of the subject, the energy with which he tends toward a future through his body and his world" (Merleau-Ponty, 1945/2012, p. 296).

However, as will be witnessed in the narratives discussed below, the phenomenology of solitary nullifies the lived experience of the "subject" and slowly erodes the possibility by which to imagine a future. Individuals often find themselves trapped in the terrifying repetition of an unchanging present that requires a constant vigilance toward the immediacy of this relentless "now." Though these individuals are able to call on a variety of strategies by which to confront the immediacy imposed by this absence, these attempts are temporary in nature and must be regularly called on to confront this experience of a never-changing manifestation of the "now" (Polizzi, 2014).

It is also important to keep in mind that though the phenomenology of solitary confinement is situated within the lived experience of those individuals held in this type of correctional isolation, it can never be exclusively viewed from that perspective. As such, this experience vividly describes a social world whose architecture and perspective is co-constituted in every aspect of its lived meaning and, as such, reflects an intentionality that is characterized by cruelty and indifference. Stated more simply, it is impossible to view these experiences outside of the socially constructed context from which they occur: a type of domination that evokes a variety of characteristics in those so dominated, which is then used to justify its continued existence.

From general population to solitary: the snare of isolation

The relationship between general modes of incarceration and the application of solitary confinement has been well known for decades. However, the transition from general population to disciplinary custody does not simply entail the relocation from one area of the penitentiary to another: Rather, this transition is more akin to suddenly finding oneself in an alien world, where most of the taken-for-granted aspects of normal experience are fundamentally disrupted. This includes the taken-for-granted understanding of penitentiary rules as they are enforced in the "normal world" of solitary confinement.

Johnny Perez reported that he entered the New York system when he was 21 after being convicted of armed robbery.

> "Within a few months that I was there, I ended up doing drugs. I tested positive for marijuana. So any misbehavior report that you receive in solitary, is going to lead to more solitary time.

Even if that initial solitary report would not send you to solitary if you were in general population. What that means is that I can be sentenced to 90 days and then catch a misbehavior report for ripping a towel in half or ripping a sheet in half to maybe create a curtain to cover the door because I want to use the bathroom…" (Johnny Perez, retrieved from *The Guardian* 6x9 Project, www.theguardian.com).

Johnny's mention of this specific aspect of solitary confinement raises one of the most important concerns related to this type of practice, particularly for individuals suffering from mental illness.

As Johnny observes, the lived space of solitary confinement is governed by a heightened sense of institutional control and regulation. Unlike the environment of general population, even the most minor infractions will result in accruing more time in disciplinary custody (Kupers, 2016). Institutional control is absolute and non-negotiable. Even the modest attempt to create some degree of normalcy while using the bathroom is now a violation of penitentiary rules. Now even the performance of specific bodily functioning is not allowed to exist outside of this totalizing panoptical perspective. He goes on to say, 'It is not uncommon to find somebody who is sentenced to a year and ends up with five, six, seven years in the box' (Johnny Perez, retrieved from *The Guardian* 6x9 Project, www.theguardian.com).

Though it is certainly true that the lived space of solitary confinement generally imposes a much more intrusive demand for compliance with prison authority, this requirement can become particularly problematic for the mentally ill inmate who is placed in disciplinary custody. Given the sparse conditions of the environment of solitary confinement, it is not at all unusual for the mentally ill inmate to rapidly decompensate. This is particularly true for the individual suffering from BPD, which is predicated on a variety of clinical criteria related to issues of abandonment, extreme fluctuations in affective experience, and a highly vulnerable formulation of the self (American Psychiatric Association, 2013).

As was discussed in Chapter one, my experience as a psychological specialist with the Pennsylvania DOC, regularly confronted the very situation which Johnny describes and which quite often can become a trap for more psychologically vulnerable inmates. In fact, I had a number of "clients" who were sent to the "hole" (the term the "box," as far as I know is used by New York and Arizona exclusively) for relatively minor infractions, but ended up accumulating years of disciplinary custody time once placed in solitary confinement. This result was particularly true for those clients suffering from BPD, who simply were psychologically unable to tolerate the pathology-inducing conditions of segregation. As a result, it was not at all unusual for an inmate to receive as much as a decade of disciplinary custody time while in solitary, far eclipsing the maximum number of years required by the individual's sentence.

One of the most immediate consequences of placing a psychologically vulnerable individual in solitary confinement is that these clients could accrue more time in segregation than the time left on their initial sentence. Though this segregation time could not be used to extend the sentence imposed by the court, it would likely mean that almost all of the remaining time left on that sentence would be served in disciplinary custody. What this generally meant in the Pennsylvania system, at least at the time that I was there, was that the individual would likely be required to "max out" their sentence. Given that an inmate is not eligible for parole in Pennsylvania while in disciplinary custody, it effectively transformed what is legally defined as an indeterminate sentence into one that would require that the individual serve the maximum amount of penitentiary time, effectively eliminating the possibility for early release. A common phrase I often heard during that time was 'The only thing you're promised is your "max",' and with this type of disciplinary strategy, it becomes guaranteed.

For the mentally ill individual or for the individual who simply can no longer bear this inhumane experience of isolation, the apparatus of solitary confinement overwhelms and shatters the self. It is important to note that this result is not simply the re-fabrication of a docile self;

rather it reflects the complete negation of the self, when all relational possibilities are systematically denied (Guenther, 2013). The narrative provided by Five Omar Mualimm is specifically relevant, insofar as he spent five years and eight months in solitary confinement.

Prior to Mualimm's placement in solitary, he had been diagnosed with bipolar disorder, but on entry into solitary, he states that his medication was discontinued! 'Lithium was the only thing I was given for my bipolar disorder. That got discontinued when I was sent into the box. It's hard when you have two personalities in your head already, so my raging came out of that' (Five Omar Mualimm, retrieved from *The Guardian* 6x9 Project, www.theguardian.com). He continues by stating 'I learned not to react to it inside, because it is only punishment, punishment, punishment. So you have to learn to curtail yourself back after years and years. It's easy to get another ticket; it's easy to get more time' (Five Omar Mualimm, retrieved from *The Guardian* 6x9 Project).

Though Mualimm does not specifically say so, it does appear to be implied that much of his solitary time was imposed after he was placed in isolation without being appropriately medicated for bipolar disorder. It would be clinically unlikely for an individual with untreated bipolar disorder not to "act out" under such conditions. It is also incredibly unethical that the psychiatric staff would allow this situation to exist and continue without intervening.

As will be seen in other interviews, many of these individuals describe bouts of severe depression, hallucinations, and obsessed thoughts, although none of these individuals entered solitary with an existing diagnosis of a chronic psychiatric disorder. The fact that an individual was placed into solitary without medication is really unspeakable and it would not be overly dramatic to call such a situation an example of extended torture. Though it does appear from Mualimm's account that after a period of time, he was able to devise a strategy by which to "control" these symptoms, how much disciplinary time was accrued and how much needless psychological suffering was experienced before this result was achieved?

Entering into the impoverished world of solitary

One of the most observed themes that was witnessed across all of these narratives was the initial experience of entering the solitary confinement unit and cell where this time would be served.

> They put you in an environment where you can't talk to anybody else, you can't have any contact … unless you scream … The only thing you get to hear is the jingling of keys … And that type of psychological imbalance you place upon somebody is very detrimental … (Rhodes, 2004, p. 31).

> "So when you first walk in the cell it's empty and it's so quiet you can hear your heart beat" (Johnny Perez, audio retrieved from *The Guardian* 6x9 Project, www.theguardian.com).

> "I remember stepping into the cell and it was like stepping over a bridge into another world" (Five Omar Mualimm, audio retrieved from *The Guardian* 6x9 Project, www.theguardian. com).

> "When you are put into solitary confinement you are taken at a moment's notice. I mean, if anything they try not to even warn you. You just feel like your whole world was ripped out from under you. It's like you have just been put into another country that you don't even know the language or the area or anything, the area you have to navigate because you have to reestablish yourself in this new world" (Dolores Canales, audio retrieved from *The Guardian* 6x9 Project, www.theguardian.com).

> "They took me from my cell down stairs and I got to the first floor, and they took me through this other door. It was like a steel door and we walked through this long hall way and I looked and there was another steel door and on the steel door it said SHU. When I stood there I could see rows of cells on both sides. I

didn't hear no noise and that was kinda strange. I was like, what is this place, it was eerie. I thought I was the only one there. It scared me" (Victor Pate, audio retrieved from *The Guardian* 6x9 Project, www.theguardian.com).

"The very first moment that I went into solitary confinement was fearful for me. It was just the fear of the unknown: you walk into this building and the lights are so dim and you can barely see, everything is so dark" (Marcel Neil, audio retrieved from *The Guardian* 6x9 Project, www.theguardian.com).

In each of these accounts, the initial experience of the unit or actual cell is recalled as something alien, something that is unknown, unusual, and clearly frightening. One's former experience of the world is disrupted due to a foreboding sense of absence: no noise, dimmed lights, no people; an alien world where one is so out of place, even its language is unavailable; a space where normal interaction is not possible. The initial experience of this phenomenology of absence seems to deny any co-constituting relationality from which a sharing of this world becomes possible. In describing the philosophical implications of this type of experience, Guenther (2013) observes that "It not only dulls the senses and impairs the cognitive faculties (as if these were two different parts of the body-mind machine) but also attacks the structure of intentional consciousness by impoverishing the world to which consciousness is essentially and irrevocably correlated" (p. 35).

As these accounts reveal, the initial experience of solitary confinement is not about resistance or any another secondary considerations; rather, it becomes solely focused on this confrontation with a world so impoverished that it becomes difficult to recognize how it can be taken up. As Guenther (2013) powerfully states, solitary confinement does not simply isolate inmates from the normal interactions, it fundamentally disrupts the relational ontology of human lived experience. This disruption of intersubjective experience, in fact, becomes a profound desubjectification of living beings, who must struggle with the apparatus of absence and the negation of normal human relating. The emergence of the subject now becomes predicated on the degree to which this in-between can be recognized and lived.

The search for relationship: the phenomenology of relationship in the absence of solitary confinement

Once the experience of solitary confinement starts to unfold from behind the steel door, these individuals begin by starting to search for strategies by which some manner of immediate relationality can be restored.

"I found myself imagining a lot. I'd talk out loud because sometimes I'd get so silent I wanted just to hear a human voice. So I might scream, I might sing, I might rap, and I might express my ideas out loud while I walk. I might create an imaginary friend that I'm talking to, just to keep me company and bounce my thoughts off of. I found that my imaginary friend would never talk back, but he was a good listener" (Johnny Perez, audio retrieved from *The Guardian* 6x9 Project, www.theguardian.com).

"I had a tree fly in my cell one day. … First I was trying to kill him and then we started to play tag. … I touched him, but it didn't hit, it didn't kill him, so I got frustrated and I laid down and he lands on my shoulder, so I say, Oh so you're playing tag right? And then, I sit back down and he's walking around and I say so you came for food. So I try to make him kinda side portion of a meal. I did not want him to leave my cell" (Five Omar Mualimm, audio retrieved from *The Guardian* 6x9 Project, www.theguardian.com).

"I read once that prisoners of war used to keep their mind by remembering things from way back; so I used to try to remember people like in my first grade class and people in my second grade class. You know, their names, things like that. Who sat behind me? The school report that I did, you know, things like that" (Dolores Canales, audio retrieved from *The Guardian* 6x9 Project, www.theguardian.com).

"Now I would often place myself in the free world with my family, with my loved ones and with my friends. I was going to school and times when I was ice skating and roller skating. Things that I did in my life at an earlier point before I got where I am ..." (Victor Pate, audio retrieved from *The Guardian* 6x9 Project, www.theguardian.com).

These reflections seem to address various strategies by which the experience of isolation can be temporarily overcome or at least made somewhat more tolerable by "restoring" some semblance of relationality from one's past (Rubin, 2015). Whether this consists of reconnecting to past relationships, the creation of a silent friend, or the opportune interaction with a fly, the need to be in relationship with someone or something remains an essential aspect of this experience. This process reflects a strategy of agentic possibility that seeks to "reframe" the meaning of this experience by "re-establishing" a variety of meaningful relationships that can be evoked by which to restore a degree of "normalcy" in the face of such extreme levels of deprivation.

Merleau-Ponty (1945/2012) makes the following observation: "We must return to the social world with which we are in contact through the simple fact of our existence, and that we inseparably bear with us prior to every objectification" (p. 379). What is explored in the above descriptions is the way in which these individuals attempt to escape from the objectifying now of solitary confinement. The social world to which they "return" is the world that existed prior to incarceration; a world which they inseparably bear and which provides them a modicum of relief and a momentary possibility for escape. Moreover, it is a return to a world that is fundamentally predicated on the potentiality of movement.

We must therefore recognize that movement itself refers to the object on the basis of a mode that is irreducible to an objective and mechanical displacement; it is familiar with the object – there is a perception within movement. It does not involve a perception distinct from it that would guide it or subsist in it in an implicit or unconsciousness way (Barbaras, 2006/1999, p. 91).

Within the context of solitary confinement, the alien nature of this environment evokes a lack of familiarity relative to its profound imposition on the potentiality for movement. Barbaras (2006/1999) continues by observing "In truth, it is *movement itself* that perceives in the sense that the object exists *for* it, in which it has meaning …" (p. 91). For these individuals, this new environment has little relationship to this object for the simple reason that it does not exist for them in any familiar way. In such a diminished perceptual world, human meaning is disrupted by the fractured nature of this relational ontology.

From the perspectives offered, each individual attempts to overcome the powerful grip of the apparatus of solitary by moving beyond, at least momentarily, the daunting demands of the criminal justice machine. Though embodied relationality is denied, this demand cannot prevent the use of more imagined strategies that can provide some temporary relief to this inhumane type of existing. The phenomenology which is evoked from these encounters is an intentional strategy by which an experience of a co-constituted relationality becomes possible, in spite of the diabolical or even psychopathic ends that seek to deny the same. In each of these strategies, an attempt is made to reconstruct a relationship to the object that is meaningful. However, certain individuals were perhaps more "successful" in their attempt to overcome the immediate circumstances of their situation then were others.

For example, Dolores Canales states that she would: 'dress up for dinner, even though I would eat right there in the cell [laughs]. I would say, you know you guys, let's put our sheets on, and let's make dresses out of our sheets. You know, just to break up the monotony' (Dolores Canales, audio retrieved from *The Guardian* 6x9 Project, www.theguardian.com). Though Canales is able to laugh at her attempt to restore a degree of normalcy around the experience of dinner, her strategy of "dressing up" does evoke the presence of an intersubjective encounter that invites the other women on the unit to re-create the space of sharing a meal with the intent of challenging the isolating event of eating alone. Her strategy not only "breaks up the monotony" of solitary, but is able to establish a co-constituted experience that can be shared by all the women involved. By so doing, she is able to re-create a degree of familiarity with the "object" of social experience that is denied by this setting. She uses this opportunity to push back against the objectifying world of disciplinary custody and re-establishes for herself and the other women on her unit a semblance of relational meaning. Now this is not to imply that such events fundamentally change the isolating reality of solitary, but such experiences do help to chip away at the overwhelming enormity of this situation.

Tyrrell Muhammad stated that while in solitary confinement at a correctional facility located in Auburn, New York, he was sent to the "box" for not being 'in front of your cell door for count, so an officer … He called the Sergeant and they hand cuffed me and they dragged me off to solitary confinement.' Once in solitary, he was given an additional six months for violating the rule for not remaining silent: He was subsequently transferred to another solitary confinement facility at another institution. On his arrival at the new facility, '…they dragged me down these steps to what they call the receiving room and there was like several other officers there and they just commenced to beating on me. They say that this is what they do to problem people here' (Tyrrell Muhammad, retrieved from *The Guardian* 6x9 Project, www.theguardian.com).

Muhammad seems to intimate that his transfer and the subsequent illegal beating that followed was related to his age. He was 20 years old at the time. He appears to reason that perhaps this direct intimidation was employed to "correct" any further "problematic behavior"; a goal which was initially successful. So successful in fact that he refused to respond to other inmates on the unit who would regularly ask him how he was doing. 'And I was afraid to talk really because what had happened at Auburn; I didn't want that to happen here.' However, he is able to break through this initial attempt to scare him into silence with the help of the other individuals on the unit.

> "But I'm still petrified to talk, but by that time I'm listening to the conversations and I'm hearing political debates, people playing chess. So you can talk here! So I called out to a guy (laughing!) hey this is three cell … Everybody got quiet. 'Oh, you finally ready to talk now huh?' I said, I didn't know you could talk up here. They said, 'we got our own set of rules.'" (Tyrrell Muhammad, audio retrieved from *The Guardian* 6x9 Project, www.theguardian.com).

In these last two reflections offered by Canales and Muhammad, an attempt is made to expand the possibility of co-constituted relationality by which to temporarily suspend the immediate limitations of their individual cells. For Canales, she is able to "reach" beyond the confines imposed by her steel door by creating a shared experience with some of the other women on the unit, which helped to lessen some of the monotony that so defined her reality. She added that the women also used singing as another way to construct an experience of relationship that helped to mitigate their social isolation. For Muhammad this same result is not so easily achieved.

The blatant use of physical aggression by which his so-called "problematic behavior" – for talking with other inmates – was addressed, had the immediate result of 'scaring him silent.' Though he was able to listen to what was being discussed on the unit, and as a result was able to establish an indirect relational space that exited outside the immediacy of his cell, he still was initially unwilling to make direct contact with these other individuals. Over time his fear subsided, which allowed him to become more actively engaged on this unit. However, after a period of time in general population, he was returned to solitary confinement, for once again being "a problem."

After Muhammad was released back into general population, he started to experience difficulty with his eyes, which appeared now to have become painfully sensitive to sunlight. 'I'm like, oh man, I need to see a doctor about my eyes. I ask to go to medical and they deny my request and then I continue to complain' (Tyrrell Muhammad, retrieved from *The Guardian* 6x9 Project, www.theguardian.com). Muhammad continued by pointing out how these requests for medical treatment were used as an example of the "problem behavior" this facility would not tolerate.

> "'Remember we told you when you came here that we were not going to tolerate problem behavior.' 'You're a trouble maker now, for advocating for yourself' and they put me right back in the box. They give me six months. Now I'm really kinda of angry because I know I'm being taken advantage of. You know, this is not right" (Tyrrell Muhammad, audio retrieved from *The Guardian* 6x9 Project, www.theguardian.com).

Muhammad says that after this unfair treatment, he contacts a federal judge and starts to begin the process to file a habeas corpus complaint against the penitentiary. During what is explained to him as a routine cell search, his legal material is discovered and is subsequently deemed to be "contraband," and he is given another 12 months in the box. As a result of this situation he reported that he fell into a deep depression and started to experience his situation as that of total helplessness. 'There is no one to hear my pleas. There's no one here to give me a fair shake. There is no one here to actually intervene. So I just went into a real depression. I became an introvert. I wouldn't eat sometimes; I didn't talk to people' (Tyrrell Muhammad, audio retrieved from *The Guardian* 6x9 Project, www.theguardian.com).

It is important to note that this current retreat into silence was not solely related to fear, but rather emerged from the place of a profound depression that threatened to swallow him up in the hopelessness it evoked. If it is possible to construct his former refusal to remain silent as a type of resistance to the subjecting demands of institutionally legitimated violence, his more recent embrace of silence was a turning away from the world and the limited relationality that it offered. In describing this experience, he stated: 'I got depressed. Some guys would try to call out to me and I wouldn't answer back. So I just, you know, turned inward. I went between crying, depression, anger. You know I went through these emotional upheavals, which I did for about fifteen months' (Tyrrell Muhammad, audio retrieved from *The Guardian* 6x9 Project, www.theguardian.com).

What Muhammad's account reveals is the fraying of the self as it begins to fall into the hopelessness of depression. Included in this process is the way in which the penitentiary machine demarcates the boundaries of the self relative to what is allowed and what is not. However, this demarcation is not simply predicated by juridical regulation; instead it reflects how this juridical strategy underlies how basic existence will be allowed to be. If similar conditions were discovered in free society their perpetrators would be viewed as monstrously criminal and their psychology psychopathic! Though Muhammad finds various ways to advocate for himself, these very attempts are what continue to evoke the ire of penitentiary power. Within this manifestation of the state of exception, the pursuit of actual justice is not allowed and is in fact punished; as a result of this process, the desubjectification of the self becomes the minimum consequence for non-compliance. More ominous is its complete annihilation.

The account offered immediately above by Muhammad mirrors the experience of many of the subjects of *The Guardian's* 6x9 Project, as well those documented by Solitary Watch and elsewhere, who also experienced the onset of various psychological issues once placed in solitary confinement, including the regular presence of hallucinations or other related "symptomology."

> I see myself slipping into somewhere I don't want to go … It is like my mind is trying to go somewhere else (Rhodes, 204, p. 147).

> I'm surrounded by men who have committed suicide and men who constantly throw feces at one another. When you're caught up in this kind of mess it rubs up on you and it has that kind

of effect that sends you off into some mental state (Wallace, 2016, p. 95).

"I did do some hallucinations and yes, I did hear voices inside my head. Things that you saw, are sometimes things that you would like to see" (Victor Pate, audio retrieved from *The Guardian* 6x9 Project, www.theguardian.com).

"Not being able to keep track of time, puts me in a space where I'm so disoriented that sometimes I question myself. I question my thinking and I question reality and I ask myself, am I developing a mental illness? …There were times when I felt very, very scared and one of my worst fears is that by losing track of time that I would not know when it was time for me to leave" (Johnny Perez, retrieved from *The Guardian* 6x9 Project, www.theguardian.com).

What these accounts reveal is the extent to which the conditions of solitary confinement can be thwarted. Though each individual employed a variety of strategies by which to subvert the punishment of isolation, they were never able to do so on a regular basis. In fact, the longer one was so confined, the less effective these strategies became at overcoming what the apparatus of solitary confinement imposed (Kupers, 2016). Given that the degree of this type of isolation is so intense and so focused on the deprivation of sensual experience and any other normalizing human interaction, the momentary reprieves enjoyed by strategies of "flight" are ultimately dragged back down into this vacant relational space.

Even during the experience of hallucinations, there are '*sometimes* things you would like to see,' but there are also those times and those images you would likely rather forget. The very border between reality and fantasy becomes so blurred that this confluence simply disappears. The experience of time or the very contemplation of one's existence is thrown into question by the numbing sameness that this absence delivers. The very fact that this space is experienced as alien terrain simply reiterates the obvious: because it is. One feels so out of place in this world because all of the most essential orientating aspects of human existence are denied.

The experience of absence, which the space of solitary confinement powerfully constructs, so disrupts our basic psychological need for relationship that these individuals employ a variety of strategies by which this relationality can be restored. When these externally located interactions become incapable of overcoming this overwhelming sense of absence, a more pathological manifestation of psychological disorder emerges and begins to fill the space ushered in by this lack.

It is also possible to observe that the onset of these psychological symptoms reflects the degree to which the materiality of the body is also disrupted or negated. In such an experience, the emptiness of solitary confinement, the literal absence of any material connection with the body, or embodied subjectivity (Merleau-Ponty, 1945/2012), places the material reality of the body into question, as a profoundly imposed limitation. The body is left without a world to embrace. As a result, the body loses its potentiality to take up the world, requiring the mind to negotiate this barren space absent of any corporal relationality.

The lingering influence of the experience of solitary confinement

The final theme that I would like to briefly explore is the lingering affects this experience has had on those who lived in solitary confinement once they returned to free society. Certain individuals shared the inability to tolerate small spaces while others described the effect solitary had on their ability to interact with other people. The sole woman in this group discussed her ability to understand her son's experience, who had been housed in solitary confinement for 14 years, and what that meant for her as a mother.

Canales describes the failings of her own father, who was incarcerated during her youth, which in turn helped to contribute to her failings as a mother to her two sons. For her, solitary evoked her own sense of personal failure, and the role that this failure has played in the lives of her sons. '... or I would think that I wish I could have been a good mom. You know, like the one thing that you think that you want to do right and you just messed it up so bad' (Dolores Canales, retrieved from *The Guardian* 6x9 Project, www.theguardian. com). From this perspective, Canales was constantly reminded of her son, and by implication her failed role as his mother, by having to endure a similar type of experience.

For others in this group, the experience of solitary confinement is described concerning how it has influenced their interactions with other people and the meaning of individual space.

"One day I panicked on the train, and had to get off at the very next stop just to go upstairs to get some air because I felt so trapped. You know there are certain things that trigger those experiences sometimes" (Tyrrell Muhammad, retrieved from *The Guardian* 6x9 Project, www.theguardian.com).

"I have to have space; I can't do small spaces at all. Put me in a small space and I flip out. Don't keep me in an elevator for a long time cause I'll find a way out of there. I'll climb out the top. Where ever I am, I'm walking around. I'm not going to stay in one spot. I cannot sit still. I cannot stand still. I cannot be in one space. I think, umm that that is the result of me being in solitary confinement. Not having the option to move around" (Victor Pate, retrieved from *The Guardian*, 6x9 Project, www. theguardian.com).

"I am who I am, not because of solitary, but despite solitary. It's the most de-humanizing that thing that you can put on a human being. I managed to find the strength to not succumb to that environment. Unfortunately, I cannot say the same for a lot of my peers" (Johnny Perez, retrieved from *The Guardian* 6x9 Project, www.theguardian.com).

"After my release from prison, the majority of things that have taken place in solitary confinement have, they really stuck with me, but the one thing that I can point out the most is being able to interact with a lot of people at one time. It's very hard for me to interact with more than two or three people at the same time without feeling somewhat paranoid or sometimes I feel like I'm having a panic attack" (Marcel Neil, retrieved from *The Guardian* 6x9 Project, www.theguardian.com).

"It took getting into a relationship and living with that person for many years to understand what solitary confinement does to a person. So physically my partner was unable to touch me on most parts of my body … for five years before we could even touch … and even to this day I don't like being, I often cringe when I get touched. Physically, literally cringe by being touched, so there is that" (Steven Czifra, retrieved from *The Guardian* 6x9 Project, www.theguardian.com).

"My son has been in solitary for fourteen years. I think that that has been the hardest part for me because I can imagine what it's like" (Dolores Canales, retrieved from *The Guardian* 6x9 Project, www.theguardian.com).

No one wants to admit that we are weak as motherfuckers that our brains beat us up. I tried to kill myself; the rope broke. I have so much survivor's guilt. I've never been involved with a woman, ever! I'm so screwed up, I don't think I can ever have a normal relationship (Nelson, 2016, p. 119).

With each of these accounts, the possibility for normal relationality has in some way been disrupted. In each description the proximity of bodily interaction has become greatly influenced and transformed by these experiences. The possibility for living movement and the meaning it evokes remains fractured and to some degree unfamiliar. For Muhammad and Pate, confined spaces become almost suffocating and evoke this need to escape; whereas for Neil, the possibility to be with too many people becomes so threatening that he can become overwhelmed with anxiety and paranoid feelings. Czifra was so effected by his experience in solitary that the touch from his partner becomes too difficult to endure. Only Perez seemed able to put this experience behind him by not allowing it to define the person he was or the person he will attempt to be. For Canales, her experience was more focused on her son, which in turn reflected for her the generational failure that directly contributed to both of their fates.

What we witness in the above narratives is the various ways in which the experience of solitary confinement fundamentally transforms the lived experience of those individuals placed in that type of correctional setting. Central to this fracturing of embodied subjectivity is the unfamiliarity of the world constructed by the practice of solitary confinement. In the absence of any significant relational interaction with other people or material objects, the very possibility for the construction of human meaning is called into question. Though numerous strategies were employed by these individuals to reconstruct some degree of intersubjective relationality, they were provisional in nature and often capable of providing only momentary relief. Even after release from the penitentiary the influence of this experience continues to linger and the taken-for-granted nature of the world remains an open question.

6
SOME CLOSING REFLECTIONS

The discussion offered in the previous chapters has attempted to explore the phenomenology of solitary confinement from the various perspectives from which these experiences are constructed. The intent of this strategy has been focused on the history and structure of solitary confinement and the ethical implications that these reveal relative to the individual experience. Though the individual experience of solitary confinement unfolds in a variety of ways, the structural context of those experiences is for the most part similar. Any attempt to explore the phenomenology of a given experience requires that both individual perspective and social context are included and the experience of solitary confinement is certainly no different.

What these experiences reveal is the way in which the apparatus of solitary confinement fundamentally disrupts and transforms some of our most basic abilities to take up the world. As a space of confinement, this experience drastically limits bodily potentiality for living movement by the absence it establishes. The emptiness of this diminished space is so pathologically vacant that the normal ways of being a person, of being a body, are effectively disrupted or at times negated. How one re-establishes some semblance of "normalcy" becomes exclusively dependent on individuals' ability to "re-inhabit" this emptiness in ways that are specifically meaningful to them. However, these experiences also evoke another aspect of this experience that is often overlooked: What does this type of confinement say about us as a society that allows its continuation?

Though it is often rationalized that solitary confinement in its most recent iteration is a necessary tool or apparatus of the criminal justice machine, we tend to continue to overlook its obvious consequences and it's more troubling ethical implications. The conditions by which solitary confinement is "strategically" employed must be viewed as an intentional act of rationalized retribution. As such, it implies an intentional desire to construct a system of punishment that elicits an intense degree of psychological harm. However, this harm rarely emerges from a place of actual hatred. Rather, and perhaps more problematically, it becomes articulated as a form of bureaucratic indifference or as the banality of evil. As a tool of institutional control, this indifference becomes rationalized as an extended consequence of the inmate's problematic behavior – those characteristics of the dominated that in turn justify unjustified domination (MacIntyre, 1988) – which threatens administrative authority and therefore must be addressed. I have been personally informed by prison administrators that ending the use of solitary could potentially threaten prison security. From this perspective, solitary confinement seeks to isolate the contagion represented by certain inmates and their behavior and by so doing provides a prophylactic intervention for other inmates and helps to insure the security of the institution.

Within this ecology of cruelty (Haney, 2008) emerges a state of exception, which reveals a psychopathic intentionality that not only is allowed to continue, but is justified as rationalized domination. Whether this is made manifest by the architectural design of such units, often so draconian in intent that even a window view of the outside world is not allowed, or by the poor ventilation that leaves the air dank and oppressive, or the dimly lit and sparse cells often punctuated by temperatures either too cold or stiflingly hot, the combined strategy is focused on the same result: to inflict as much psychological harm as possible.

Much like the sadistic perpetrator who confines and tortures their victims, solitary confinement emerges from the same psychological space that makes such action possible. Such strategies of total control and indifference when applied by the sadist are viewed as psychopathic and criminal, but when this mindset, albeit employed in a slightly revised form, becomes situated within the state of exception, exemplified by the criminal justice machine, what was formerly reprehensible now becomes justifiable, and not so unusual. Now it may be argued that such a comparison is unfair or overly dramatic, ill-informed, or simply naïve relative to the specific context in which the practice of solitary confinement occurs. After all, no one is actually being physically tortured. But as the practice of solitary confinement has clearly revealed, cruelty is still possible without the need for delivering an actual physical blow. There are many ways by which to employ a strategy of violence and many ways by which to rationalize the continued use of such practices.

Though the practice of solitary confinement does not generally include an actual torturer, the conditions are such that there is no actual necessity for an individual to inflict the requisite degree of intended harm; in the evolved manifestation of the same, this practice gains its power through an institutional process of addition by subtraction. Within this manifestation of the state of exception, there is not only a blurring of the lines of demarcation between the political order and the law, but also a blurring of the humanity of those individuals trapped within these borders.

References

Agamben, G. (2015/2014). *The use of bodies.* A. Kotsko (Trans.). Stanford, CA: Stanford University Press.

Agamben, G. (2007/2009). *What is an apparatus? And other essays.* D. Kishik & S. Pedatell (Trans.). Stanford, CA: Stanford University Press.

Agamben, G. (2005/2003). *State of exception.* K. Attell (Trans.). Chicago, IL: University of Chicago Press.

Agamben, G. (1995/1998). *Homo sacer: Sovereign power and bae life.* D. Heller-Roazen (Trans.). Stanford, CA: Stanford University Press.

APA (American Psychiatric Association) (2013). *Desk reference to the diagnostic criteria from DSM-5.* Arlington, VA: American Psychiatric Association.

Arendt, H. (2006). *Eichmann in Jerusalem: Report on the banality of evil.* New York, NY: Penguin Classics.

Arrigo, B. & Bersot, H. (2014). The case of Guantanamo Bay. In B. Arrigo & H. Bersot, *The handbook of international crime and justice studies* (pp. 256–278). London, UK & New York, NY: Routledge.

Arrigo, B., Bersot, H. & Sellers, B. (2011). *The ethics of total confinement: A critique of madness, citizenship and social justice.* Oxford, UK: Oxford University Press.

Arrigo, B.A. & Trull, S.L. (2015). History of imprisonment. In K.L. Appelbaum, J.L. Metzner, and R.L. Trestman (eds.), *The Oxford textbook of correctional psychiatry* (pp. 3–7). New York, NY: Oxford University Press.

Arrigo, B. & Milovanovic, D. (2009). *Revolution in penology: Rethinking the society of captives*. Lanham, MD: Rowman & Littlefield.

Barbaras, R. (1999/2006). *Desire and distance: Introduction to a phenomenology of perception*. P. Milan (Trans.). Stanford, CA: Stanford University Press.

Binelli, M. (2015, March, 26). Inside America's toughest federal prison. *The New York Times*. Retrieved from http://www.nytimes.com.

Bosworth, M. & Carrabine, E. (2001). Reassessing resistance: Race, gender, and sexuality in prison. *Punishment and Society*, 3, 501–515.

Carrabine, E. (2004). *Power, discourse and resistance*. Farnham, Surrey: Ashgate.

Crewe, B. (2014). The emotional geography of prison life. *Theoretical Criminology*, 18, 56–74.

Crewe, B. (2011). Depth, weight, tightness: Revisiting the pains of imprisonment. *Punishment & Society*, 13, 509–529.

Crewe, B. (2007). Power, adaptation and resistance in a late-modern men's prison. *British Journal of Criminology*, 47, 256–275.

de la Durantaye, L. (2009). *Giorgio Agamben: A critical introduction*. Stanford, CA: Stanford University Press.

Death Penalty Information Center. (2016). Retrieved from the internet 11/19/2016. http://www.deathpenaltyinfo.org/part-i-history-death-penalty.

Dey, E. (2015). Going to the Hole in California: Cauldron of solitude. In S. Richards (ed.), *The Marion experiment: Long-term solitary confinement & the supermax movement* (pp. 59–68). Carbondale, IL: Southern Illinois University Press.

Ek, R. (2006). Giorgio Agamben and the spatialities of the camp: An introduction. *Swedish Society for Anthropology and Geography*, 88, 363–386.

Foucault, M. (1977/1995). *Discipline and punish*. New York, NY: Vintage Books.

Ginwalla, A. (1992). Proportionality and the Eighth Amendment: And their object not sublime, make the punishment fit the crime. *Missouri Law Review*, 57, 607–627.

REFERENCES

Goffman, I. (1961). *Asylums: Essays on the social situation of mental patients and other inmates*. New York, NY: Anchor Books.

Goldman, D. & Brimmer, R. (2016). U.S. Supreme Court Cases. Retrieved from http://solitarywatch.com/resources/u-ssupreme-court-cases/

Gregory, D. (2006). The black flag: Guantanamo Bay and the space of exception. *Swedish Society for Anthropology and Geography*, 88, 405–427.

Gulli, B. (2007). The ontology and politics of exception: Reflections on the work of Giorgio Agamben. In M. Calarco & S. DeCaroli (eds.), *Giorgio Agamben: Sovereignty & life* (pp. 219–242). Stanford, CA: Stanford University Press.

Guenther, L. (2013). *Solitary confinement: Social death and its afterlives*. Minneapolis, MN: University of Minnesota Press.

Haney, C. (2012). Prison effects of in the age of mass incarceration. *Prison Journal*, 1–24 DOI: 10.1177/0032885512448604.

Haney, C. (2009, January). The social psychology of isolation: Why solitary confinement is psychologically harmful. *Prison Service Journal*, 1, 12–20.

Haney, C. (2008). A culture of harm: Taming the dynamics of cruelty in supermax prisons. *Criminal Justice and Behavior*, 35, 956–984.

Haney, C. (2003). Mental health issues in long-term solitary and "supermax" confinement. *Crime & Delinquency*, 49, 124–156.

Haney, C., Weill, J., Bakhshay, S. & Lockett, T. (2016). Examining jail isolation: What we don't know can be profoundly harmful. *The Prison Journal*, 96, 126–152.

Hartman, K. (2008). Supermax prisons in the consciousness of prisoners. *Prison Journal*, 88, 169–176.

Heidegger, M. (2010/1953). *Being and time*. J. Stambaugh & D. Schmidt (Trans.). Albany, NY: SUNY Press.

Immarigeon, R. (2015). Colorado supermax study: What the critics say and the future holds. In S. Richards (ed.), *The Marion experiment: Long-term solitary confinement & the supermax movement* (pp.160–174). Carbondale, IL: Southern Illinois University Press.

Kauffman, S. (2010). *The reinvention of the sacred: A new view of science.* New York, NY: Basic Books.

Kooistra, P. (1989). *Criminals as heroes: Structure, power & identity.* Bowling Green, OH: Bowling Green State University Popular Press.

Kupers, T. (2016). How to create madness in prison. In J. Casella, J. Ridgeway & S. Shourd (eds.), *Hell is a very small place: Voices from solitary confinement* (pp. 161–177). New York, NY: The New Press.

Kupers, T. (2014). Isolated confinement: Effective method for behavior change or punishment for punishment's sake. In B. Arrigo & T. Ward (Eds.), *The handbook of international crime and justice studies* (pp. 213–232). London, UK & New York, NY: Routledge.

Lanier, M., Polizzi, D. & Wade, A. (2014). Addressing the "inherent" philosophical and operational dichotomies of corrections from an EpiCrim approach. In B. Arrigo & H. Bersot (Eds.), *The handbook of international crime and justice studies* (pp. 565–584). London, UK & New York, NY: Routledge.

Levin, M. (2014). It's time to reform solitary confinement in the BOP and everywhere else it's used, too. *Corrections Managers' Report,* Vol. XIX, 81–92.

Levinas, E. (1961/1969). *Totality or Infinity.* Pittsburgh, PA: Duquesne University Press.

MacIntyre, A. (1988). *Whose justice? Which rationality?* Notre Dame, IN: University of Notre Dame Press.

Mears, D.P. & Reisig, M.D. (2006). The theory and practice of supermax prisons. *Punishment & Society*, 8, 33–57.

Merleau-Ponty, M. (1945/2012). *Phenomenology of perception.* London, UK & New York, NY: Routledge.

Minor, K & Baumgardner, M. (2015). Theorizing "Marionization" and the supermax prison movement. In S. Richards (ed.), *The Marion experiment: Long-term solitary confinement & the supermax movement* (pp. 101–114). Carbondale, IL: Southern Illinois University Press.

Murray, A. (2010). *Giorgio Agamben.* London, UK & New York, NY: Routledge.

Nelson, B. (2016). Weak as motherfuckers. In J. Casella, J. Ridgeway & S. Shourd (eds.), *Hell is a very small place: Voices from solitary confinement* (pp. 117-120). New York, NY: The New Press.

Newbold, G. (2015). Foreword: The phenomenon of USP Marion. In S. Richards (ed.), *The Marion experiment: Long-term solitary confinement & the supermax movement* (vii–ix). Carbondale, IL: Southern Illinois University Press.

O'Donnell, I. (2016). The survival secrets of solitaries. *The Psychologist*, 29, 184–187.

O'Donnell, I. (2014). Time and isolation as performance art: A note. *Crime, Media, Culture*, 10, 81–86.

O'Keefe, M. (2007). Administrative segregation for mentally ill inmates. *Journal of Offender Rehabilitation,* 45, 149–165. Pizarro, J.M. & Narag, R.E. (2008). Supermax prisons: What we know, what we do not know, and where we are going. *The Prison Journal*, 88, 23–42.

Pizarro, J. & Stenius, V.M.K. (2004). Supermax prisons: Their rise, current practices, and effects on inmates. *The Prison Journal*, 84, 248-264.

Polizzi, D. (2016). *A philosophy of the social construction of crime*. Bristol, UK: Policy Press.

Polizzi, D. (2014). Developing therapeutic trust with court-ordered clients. In D. Polizzi, M. Braswell & M. Draper (eds.), *Transforming corrections: Humanistic approaches to corrections and offender treatment* (pp.303–333). Durham, NC: Carolina Academic Press.

Polizzi, D., Draper, M. & Andersen, M. (2014). Fabricated selves and the rehabilitation machine: Toward a phenomenology of the social construction of offender treatment. In B. Arrigo & T. Ward (Eds.), *The handbook of international crime and justice studies* (pp. 233–255). London, UK & New York, NY: Routledge.

Rhodes, L. (2004). *Total confinement: Madness and reason in the maximum security prison*. Berkeley & Los Angeles, CA: University of California Press.

Richards, S. (2015). *The Marion experiment: Long-term solitary confinement & the supermax movement*. (Ed). Carbondale, IL: Southern Illinois University Press.

Richards, S. (2008). USP Marion: The first federal supermax. *The Prison Journal*, 88, 6–22.

Riveland, C. (1999). *Supermax prisons: Overview and general considerations*. Longmont, CO: US Department of Justice, National Institute of Justice.

Rothman, D. (2002). *Conscience and convenience: The asylum and its alternatives in progressive America*. New York, NY: Aldine Transaction.

Rovner, L. (2016). Solitary confinement and the law. In J. Casella, J. Ridgeway & S. Shourd (eds.), *Hell is a very small place: Voices from solitary confinement* (pp. 179–194). New York, NY: The New Press.

Rubin, A.T. (2015). Resistance or friction: Understanding the significance of prisoners' secondary adjustments. *Theoretical Criminology*, 19, 23–42.

Scull, A. (2006). *The insanity of place/the place of insanity: Essays on the history of psychiatry*. New York, NY: Routledge.

Sellin, T. (1970). The origin of the "Pennsylvania" system of prison discipline. *The Prison Journal*, 50, 13–21.

Shalev, S. (2011). Solitary confinement and the supermax prisons: A human rights and ethical analysis. *Journal of Forensic Psychology Practice*, 11, 151–183.

Shalev, S. (2009). *Supermax: Controlling risk through solitary confinement*. Cullompton, UK: Willan Publishing.

Smith, P. (2008). "Degenerate Criminals:" Mental health and psychiatric studies of Danish prisoners in solitary confinement, 1870–1920. *Criminal Justice and Behavior*, 35, 1048–1064.

Smith, P. (2004). A religious technology of the self: Rationality and religion in the rise of the modern penitentiary. *Punishment & Society*, 6, 195–220.

Suedfeld, P. & Roy, C. (1975). Using social isolation to change the behavior of disruptive inmates. *International Journal of Offender Therapy and Comparative Criminology*, 19, 90–99.

Taylor, J. M. (2015). The politicization of the Hole in Indiana and Missouri. In S. Richards (ed.), *The Marion experiment: Long-term solitary confinement & the supermax movement* (pp. 21–34). Carbondale, IL: Southern Illinois University Press.

Toch, H. (2003). The contemporary relevance of early experiments with supermax reform. *The Prison Journal*, 83, 221–228.

Toch, H. (1992). *Mosaic of despair: Human breakdowns in prison.* Washington, D.C.: American Psychological Association.

Wallace, H. (2016). Dream house. In J. Casella, J. Ridgeway & S. Shourd (Eds.), *Hell is a very small place: Voices from solitary confinement* (pp. 93–99). New York, NY: The New Press.

Ward, D.A. & Werlich, T.G. (2003). Alcatraz and Marion: Evaluating super-maximum custody. *Punishment & Society*, 5, 53–75.

Weber, M. (1978). *Economy and Society*. Los Angeles, CA: University of California Press.

Wedekind, J. (2011). Fact sheet: Solitary confinement and the law. Solitary Watch, retrieved from www.solitarywatch.com.

Supreme Court and federal appellate cases

Atkins v. Virginia, 536 U.S. 304 (2002)

Brooks v. Florida, 389 U.S. 413 (1967)

Furman v. Georgia, 408 U.S. 238 (1972)

Gregg v. Georgia, 428 U.S. 153 (1976)

In re Kemmler, 136 U.S. 436 (1890)

In re Medley, 134 U.S. 160 (1890)

Madrid v. Gomez, 889 F.Supp. 1146, 1264 (N.D. Cal 1995)

Martin v. Hadix, 527 U.S. 343 (1999)

McElvaine v. Brush, 142 U.S. 155 (1891)

O'Neil v. Vermont, 144 U.S. 323 (1898)

Pervear v. The Commonwealth, 72 U.S. 5 Wall. 475 (1866)

Roper v. Simmons, 543 U.S. 551 (2005)

Ruiz v. Johnson, 178 F.3d 385 95th Cir. 1999)

Sandin v. Conner, 515 U.S. 472 (1995)

Stanford v. Kentucky, 492 U.S. 369 (1989)

Thompson v. Oklahoma, 487 U.S. 815 (1987)

Weems v. U.S., 217 U.S. 349 (1910)

Wilkinson v. Austin, 545 U.S. 209 (2005)

Wilson v. Seiter, 501 U.S. 294 (1991)

Wolff v. McDonnell, 418 U.S. 539 (1974)

Woodson v. North Carolina, 428 U.S. 280 (1976)

Index

U

W

Z